Sutherland Smith MarketMind

Sutherland Smith MarketMind

From start-up to global player and the
people who made it happen

Tom Valenta

Copyright © 2019 Tom Valenta

First published in Australian 2019.
All rights reserved. No part of this book may be reproduced or transmitted in any form or by any means, electronic or mechanical, including photocopying, recording, or by any information storage and retrieval system without the written permission of the author, except where permitted by law.

This book is not intended to provide personalised, legal, financial or investment advice. The author and the publisher specifically disclaim any liability, loss or risk which is incurred as a consequence, directly or indirectly, of the use and application of any content of this work.

Photography offered and supplied for this publication is provided with permission to use and does not have any known royalties or copyright. The publisher and the author are held harmless from and against any and all claims, liability, losses, costs and expenses.

Publishing Details
Title: From start-up to global player - The history of Sutherland Smith/MarketMind and the people who made it happen

Editor: Pickawoowoo Publishing Group, Eddie Albrecht

Interior and cover layout: Pickawoowoo Publishing Group

Print and Distribution: Lightning Source / Ingram

A catalogue record for this book is available from the National Library of Australia

ISBN 978-0-6486871-0-8 (hardback)
ISBN 5 978-0-6486871-1-5 (paperback)

Contents

Author's Note · vii

1 When Sutherland Met Smith · 1
2 The Boy From Creswick · 5
3 The Boy From Maitland · 17
4 The De Facto Partnership · 27
5 The Continous Tracking Evolution · · · · · · · · · · · · · · · 34
6 Reforms of The 1980s · 46
7 Sutherland Smith – and Ringham · · · · · · · · · · · · · · · · 50
8 How Effective is Your Advertising? · · · · · · · · · · · · · · · 56
9 A Growing Team · 63
10 Going Global · 69
11 The Column that Became a Book · · · · · · · · · · · · · · · · 80
12 The Data Processing Revolution · · · · · · · · · · · · · · · · · 84
13 Peggy's Boiler Room · 92
14 Selling the Businesses · 98
15 After Sutherland Smith · 104
16 The Reflections of Others · 113

Acknowledgements · 125
Further Reading · 127
Endnotes · 129

Author's Note

Max Sutherland and Bruce Smith impacted market research in Australia and in many parts of the world. They helped pioneer, from the 1980s, the concept of continuous tracking research. It was the pre-internet era when even the most sophisticated consumer goods and services companies had only researched their markets on an annual or bi-annual basis. With continuous tracking, organisations could identify and better understand the effectiveness of their advertising, the impacts of competitor activity, changes in the business and consumer environments, the effectiveness of media and other significant dynamics. The pair also undertook qualitative research which set new standards in emerging areas such as investor relations and information technology.

I first met Bruce in 1982. I was working with Mayne Nickless, then a large public-listed freight transport and security company based in Melbourne. The head of our computer services division wanted to commission some market research and asked me to find a research firm that had knowledge of the emerging telecommunications and information technology sectors. At that time, our company's computer services were limited to computerised payroll – a service that was rapidly making old-style, cash-filled pay packets obsolete. The division's desire was to expand into new markets.

A former colleague who was a market researcher recommended Smith & Sharp. He told me that Bruce was an outstanding researcher and that he had recently taken on a new partner, Kevin Sharp, who had been a market researcher with Telecom, the forerunner of Telstra. It was an ideal choice. At our first meeting, the head of our computer services division gave Bruce and Kevin one simple task: 'I want you to research something that I know will be big in the future, it's called electronic mail.' He wanted to understand how quickly this new service would emerge. Based on the research findings, he would decide whether Mayne Nickless should invest in electronic mail.

The findings were simple and accurate – yes electronic mail was going to be a huge industry, but not for some years. The work was impressive, and it formed the basis of an ongoing relationship with Mayne Nickless even though the company did not invest in the future technology. A year later, Bruce advised me that he and Kevin had decided to go their separate ways and I was introduced to his new partner, Max Sutherland. A new research firm, Sutherland Smith had been formed. Soon after, they launched a new business venture known as continuous tracking which they later named MarketMind and it became a global enterprise. There were to be other initiatives, including the new field of investor relations. This came about with the deregulation of the Australian financial sector from 1983 to 1987. Sutherland Smith quickly grasped the intricacies of financial markets and provided outstanding qualitative and quantitative research to listed companies, including those planning mergers and acquisitions.

In the mid-1990s I was planning to establish a business partnership and I turned to Bruce and Max for advice. The history of partnerships was littered with failures and yet theirs was clearly very successful. What could I learn? The guidance they gave me was priceless. My intended partner and I set up what they had done a decade earlier and had called it a 'de facto partnership'. From our arrangement that copied the Bruce and Max model, my de facto partner and I learned we were not compatible in business despite our personal friendship. As a result, no formal arrangement ensued. The de facto concept that Bruce and Max implemented is covered in Chapter 4 and should be mandatory reading for anyone planning a new business partnership. It could save potential partners much heartache and considerable financial distress.

Over the years, the business relationship I had with Sutherland Smith grew into much more. Personal friendships flourished with both Bruce and Max and our families. I had the great pleasure of taking Bruce to a corporate box at the MCG

AUTHOR'S NOTE

to watch his beloved Richmond Tigers play. And by sheer coincidence his son, Paul, and my younger son, Leigh, attended the same judo academy. With Max I shared an interest in writing and current affairs. I enjoyed the column he wrote for the advertising and marketing trade journal *AdNews* and, along with other friends, encouraged him to write a book based on these illuminating columns. *Advertising and the Mind of the Consumer: what works, what doesn't and why* was first published in 1993 and there were to be three international editions over the following two decades. The columns and the book are detailed in Chapter 11.

Long after Max and Bruce sold their businesses, we have remained friends. Max spent time lecturing at universities in the United States before returning to Australia in 2001. He came back to Melbourne and wrote a blog until 2010. He was also a part-time consultant and adjunct professor at Swinburne, Bond and Monash universities. Max was also actively involved in Dying with Dignity Victoria (DWDV), a not-for-profit organisation dedicated to promoting humane end-of-life options as well as changing the law on assisted dying. Inspired by Max, I became a member of DWDV in 2009 when my wife Marie was near the end of her life. The support of DWDV helped me cope with my most tragic time.

Bruce, in addition to his commitments to the Richmond Football Club, has provided his professional skills to the Scanlon Foundation. It was established in 2001 by businessman and philanthropist Peter Scanlon to enhance and foster social cohesion in Australia. Bruce has also made a significant contribution to surf lifesaving in Victoria. The immense contributions they have both made after the Sutherland Smith days are detailed in Chapter 15.

To write the Sutherland Smith story is a great privilege and pleasure. There is always much to be learned from history, even when it covers a recent and familiar period. The era covered in this book was one of remarkable change in Australia and internationally, and to look back is a fascinating journey.

Tom Valenta
2019

1

When Sutherland Met Smith

Bruce Smith and Max Sutherland have differing recollections of when they first met. Bruce recalls it being at a regular, Friday-evening social get-together of tenants at a building they shared in Jolimont Terrace, an historic precinct in Melbourne's Yarra Park and a short walk from the Melbourne Cricket Ground (MCG). The building, known as Coningsby, was completed in 1882 and was briefly the residence of Melbourne entrepreneur James Garton. One hundred years later, all the tenants were self-employed market researchers. The specific time and date of that meeting are long forgotten but by process of deduction, it must have been in the early 1980s. They both believe it was at least one year before they decided to work together.

The building where Bruce and Max first worked together.

At that first get-together, Max was advocating for continuous tracking research and what he was saying impressed Bruce. Both recognised that 'point-in-time' research was outdated and that markets were changing rapidly. For companies to truly understand their consumers, a new approach to research was required. That very first conversation was, as Bruce described it, 'a light bulb moment for me.'

Bruce Smith and Max Sutherland

For Max, his recollection of his first encounter with Bruce was a little earlier. From the early 1980s, Bruce was editing a recently launched newsletter for the Victorian division of the Market Research Society of Australia (MRSA). In later years the MRSA became the Australian Market and Social Research Society (AMSRS). Max, who had been lecturing at the Caulfield Institute of Technology, was on the MRSA's state committee and was impressed with Bruce's work. At a function of the society, Max made a point of seeking out Bruce and complimenting him on the quality of the newsletter. It was a fleeting encounter, not long before their conversation at Jolimont Terrace.

Australia's population at the beginning of the 1980s was around 14.7 million, Melbourne's population was nearing 2.8 million and Sydney's was more than 3.2 million. The era heralded some key innovations in science, technology and other areas that would have immense and enduring impacts on all sectors of the economy including market research. In 1980 the first commercial FM radio stations were launched in mainland capital cities. A year later the major banks introduced the nation's first automatic teller machines (ATMs) which were progressively rolled out – an early example of artificial intelligence. The personal computer market began to boom in the early part of the decade with Apple and IBM being the driving forces. And the facsimile machine, hooked up to telephone lines, became a new and rapid method for businesses, government departments and other organisations to communicate locally and globally.

In addition to their research interests, Bruce and Max had some personal background in common. Both were born in regional towns – Max in New South Wales, Bruce in Victoria. Both lost their fathers very early and had overcome hardships as a result.

Their professional careers were somewhat different. Bruce had two previous business partnerships that had not worked out while Max liked to shuttle between business and academia. Bruce had worked at HJ Heinz and a large advertising agency, Masius Wynne-Williams, in Melbourne, London and Pretoria before launching an independent market research company with the first of his partners in 1977.

Max lectured in academia in Sydney, Melbourne and the United States of America. While lecturing at the University of NSW, one of his students, in partnership with Max, started a market research company in Sydney. After 18 months Max resigned from the university to run the company full-time. But he soon became bored with the CEO role and sold the company, taking up a role as Market Research Manager for the Overseas Telecommunications Commission (OTC). A year later he returned to teaching, moving to Caulfield Institute of Technology in Melbourne. Four years later he shuffled back to business with a 12-month stint co-managing the Melbourne office of McNair Anderson before again going out on his own as a sole trader. After studying marketing, and then psychology, he eventually completed a master's and then a doctorate in psychology.

Their differences were many, and as such they complemented each other's strengths and weaknesses. Even their divergent personalities synchronised well. Bruce's strong team sport history and thorough post-commerce degree training at Heinz and the lengthy periods served in the advertising industry had developed his gregarious style and ability to sell, and gave him the physical resilience to put in long days and years at the office. He understood how to work as part of a team and could see that Max's academic temperament required time for thought and contemplation and the freedom to meet like minds.

One difference was the emphasis of their research focus. Most of Max's work was quantitative research while Bruce's was largely qualitative. What are the differences? Quantitative research is based on the collection of large quantities of data from wide representative samples of the populations that can be extrapolated to the total population. Originally conducted either by door-to-door interviewing or self-completion mailed questionnaires, today the quantitative data collection is mostly obtained by telephone (both fixed line and mobile) and online surveys. Quantitative data collection methods are much more structured than qualitative research and the emphasis is on being able to reliably measure and replicate survey results. Examples include measuring market share of competing products and services, determining voting patterns or intentions, and assessing the effectiveness of advertising campaigns as well as community conditions such as social cohesion. Historically, quantitative surveys were conducted at specific points in time, and while capable of reliably measuring events at those specific points in time, they were unreliable predictors of future trends. Continuous tracking, which measured events on an ongoing basis, was the missing link which enabled users to more accurately understand market movements and predict future trends.

Qualitative research is generally defined as exploratory, highly targeted, probing research designed to gain an understanding of underlying factors and motivations which drive and/or explain attitudes, behaviours and beliefs. The data is generally collected through focus groups, one-on-one interviews and other tailored methods. It does not seek to be representative but rather identify key drivers of societal behaviours.

The two methodologies are generally complementary, and in many cases organisations will undertake both to gain knowledge and understanding of their markets and wider societal attitudes and behaviours. In most cases, the qualitative work is done first followed by the quantitative. The qualitative work identifies key issues and the quantitative determines the extent of the issues.

2

THE BOY FROM CRESWICK

Bruce Edmund Smith was born in the Victorian country town of Creswick on June 28, 1944. Creswick, which is 18km north of Ballarat, was established during the Victorian gold rush era of the 1850s and was named after three pioneering brothers who farmed in the area, Henry, Charles and John Creswick. It is also the birthplace in 1885 of John Curtin who was Australia's Prime Minister from 1941 to 1945.

Tragedy struck the Smith family soon after Bruce's birth. His father Edmund William Elphick Smith, who worked in a local timber mill, was killed at the age of 31 in an industrial accident when Bruce was only six weeks old. The year of 1944 was a dismal one for the entire Smith family. The war in the Pacific was still raging and two of Edmund's three brothers were serving in the Australian

The boy from Creswick (left) training with another Richmond recruit, Brian McMillan.

Army. One had been captured when Singapore fell to the Japanese in early 1942 and two years later his fate was still unknown. It was only at the war's end in 1945 that he was found to be alive having survived working as a prisoner on the notorious Burma Railway. Another was posted to Darwin during the 1942-43 Japanese air-raids and a third brother had taken his own life in 1944. In later years, Bruce often reflected on how his grandfather, a widower, must have felt at a time when he had cause to believe he might have lost all four sons.

Bruce's mother, Amelia Grace Krause, was one of four children born to a mother of Cornish and father of German origin. Known always by her second name, Grace was raised in the Wimmera region. She met Edmund in Maryborough, a small town in central Victoria mid-way between Ballarat and Bendigo. They married in Creswick and settled there. Meanwhile her parents moved to Melbourne and ran milk bars in inner suburban Richmond and North Melbourne before moving to Black Rock in the south-eastern bayside region. They then built a house in nearby Sandringham to where they retired.

Grace and her son stayed in Creswick until 1950. Money was scarce, so she took in schoolteachers as boarders to supplement her small workers' compensation pension. Eventually they moved to Sandringham to live with her parents. The move to the city fired Bruce's love of Australian Rules Football. To this day, the first birthday gift he vividly recalls receiving was a football!

'My mother's brother, Alan Krause, was on the senior list at the Melbourne Football Club, so we were always attending matches, mostly reserves grade. Naturally I became a passionate Demons' supporter, which at the time was a dream ride.' The 1950s were a golden era for the club and it won four premierships during that decade.

Through her Wimmera connections, Grace was friendly with a farming family and spent several weeks each year helping at shearing time. These trips coincided with school holidays, so Bruce went with her to stay on the property near Wal Wal, a tiny farming settlement between Stawell and Horsham.

On one of these trips, Grace met Mick Simmons, a returned serviceman and brother of the farmer's wife. A romance flourished, they married in 1954 and Grace and Bruce moved from the city to Wal Wal. The couple had a son, John in 1956.

Bruce recalls leaving East Sandringham Primary School where average class sizes were 30 to a school with a total population of 11 children. After completing his primary schooling, Bruce started his secondary education at Stawell technical school where, in his first year, he was dux of his class. However, Wal Wal was a temporary home as his stepfather was waiting to be allocated a soldier settlement farm. This was a scheme that commenced after the First World War and was refined after the Second World War. The scheme utilised both Crown lands and established properties which were acquired and broken up into smaller allotments enabling returned servicemen to gain inexpensive entry to the rural sector. The Simmons' farm was made available in late 1956 and in February 1957 the family moved to Telangatuk East, another tiny farming community between Horsham and Hamilton in the Western District. It was at a Christmas party at the end of 1957 where Bruce met Sue Dunstan, the daughter of another local farming family. Bruce was 13 and Sue was 11 and her memory from that day is seeing a very tall boy with a toddler happily draped over his shoulder. The toddler was Bruce's half-brother, John.

Bruce's secondary schooling continued at yet another small settlement, Balmoral. He travelled there on a school bus and one of his fellow travellers was Sue Dunstan. Sue's family had recently moved from the Mallee to Telangatuk East. The Dunstan family was related to the former Premier of Victoria, Sir Albert Dunstan, who had been a farmer before a long political career that included two spells as premier in the 1930s and 1940s.

They both attended Balmoral Consolidated School which only taught students to Year 8. Bruce fulfilled his youthful ambition when he became captain of the school football team. He was also selected to represent South West Victoria at the 1958 State Under-15 football championships.

After finishing Year 9 at Balmoral by correspondence, Bruce had to find another school to complete his secondary education. An aunt who was a mathematics teacher in Melbourne had taken an interest in his education and arranged for Bruce to enrol at Hampton High School where she taught. Hampton borders Sandringham so Bruce was able to live with his grandparents while getting his matriculation certificate. Meanwhile, Sue went to Horsham to continue her education.

It was a time of mixed emotions for Bruce: 'I recall this period in my life as a difficult and challenging time, adjusting to higher education standards, making new friends and living away from my family, especially my mother, for the first time. By this time, I had a half-brother and recall experiencing some feelings of alienation from the family. Fortunately, I had caring grandparents and was also able to pursue my two loves, football and cricket.'

He initially played football with the Black Rock Under-17 team and then cricket, also for the neighbouring suburb of Black Rock. The then captain of the cricket club's first XI was Don Chipp who, from 1960, sat in Federal Parliament as the Liberal Party member for Higginbotham. Chipp had a long, high-profile and somewhat controversial political career. He was a minister in the governments led by Harold Holt, John Gorton and William McMahon but later fell out with his party. In 1977 he was elected to the Senate as the leader of a new party he created, the Australian Democrats. He served in this role until 1986 and died in 2006 aged 81.

While still at school, Bruce – tall and athletic – attracted the interests of teams in the Victorian Football League (VFL). He had been made captain of the Hampton High School senior team succeeding Ross Smith (no relation) who was to become a champion St Kilda footballer and winner of the 1967 Brownlow Medal. In 1961 Bruce won the school's best and fairest award and the Hampton Rovers Under-19s best and fairest. Both were awarded by the St Kilda football club. It was a stellar year for Bruce, he was also selected in the combined high schools' representative team and the Victorian Amateur Under-19 team.

After gaining his matriculation certificate and a Commonwealth scholarship in 1961, Bruce went to the University of Melbourne in 1962 where, three years later, he attained a degree in commerce. That year his football career also blossomed. In those years, VFL clubs' recruitment programs were restricted by a zoning system with each club allocated a specific geographic zone. For aspiring young footballers living in Sandringham and other bayside suburbs, this meant they were in St Kilda's zone. But Bruce successfully argued that his permanent home was Telangatuk East which was not allocated to a specific club and therefore he was free to go to one of his choice. His high school economics teacher was a passionate Richmond fan and he had urged Bruce to join the Tigers. It was Richmond that showed most interest in him so, from 1962, Bruce played in the Under-19s, reserves and senior teams. He became a devoted Tiger supporter even though his elite football career there was relatively short. AFL football and its networks were to be influential throughout his business career.

In 1966, Bruce joined the global food processing and marketing giant HJ Heinz as a graduate trainee. It was the year that Sir Robert Menzies retired as prime minister after 16 years in the role – a record that still stands. He was succeeded by Harold Holt who had been a cabinet minister since 1949 but spent less than two years as prime minister having disappeared and presumed drowned while swimming near Point Nepean in December 1967.

Australia's population in 1966 was just over 11.5 million. Australian troops, including conscripts, were fighting in Vietnam while on the domestic scene, decimal currency was introduced – dollars and cents replaced pounds, shillings and pence.

Bruce left the Richmond Football Club at the end of 1965 and played with Dandenong in the Victorian Football Association in 1966 and '67. As Heinz was based in the industrial suburb of Dandenong, Bruce was easily able to get to training sessions. After two seasons, culminating in the 1967 VFA premiership, he decided to end his football career.

At Heinz he worked in several departments including finance, personnel and marketing. It was when he was assigned to market research that he envisioned a future career. Heinz was at the cutting edge of product marketing and was heavily committed to researching its markets.

Meanwhile, Bruce and his school-days sweetheart, Sue Dunstan, were reunited. They had maintained a correspondence and saw each other when Bruce returned to Telangatuk East during school and university holidays. Together they attended a Smith family wedding in Stawell. Sue was 17 and Bruce 19. This was the beginning of their relationship which flourished when Sue came to Melbourne in 1964 to do nurse's training at the Alfred Hospital. They married in 1968 and celebrated their 50th anniversary as this book was being written.

After four years at Heinz, Bruce decided to specialise and found himself a position in a market research agency. He joined Marplan, a firm headed by Brian Sweeney who was to become one of Australia's best-known and highly respected researchers. However, within months of Bruce joining the firm, Sweeney left and went to live and work in the UK. The loss of Sweeney, who later returned to establish his own firm, was a huge setback for Marplan and it struggled to replace him.

In 1970, after only a year with Marplan, Bruce joined the large, high-profile advertising agency, Masius Wynn-Williams as research manager. Known in the industry simply as Masius, its clients included Qantas, Mobil, Toyota, Wilkinson Sword, ACI (Australian Consolidated Industries), Julius Marlow shoes, Tarax beverages and the Mars confectionery group which also owned Uncle Ben's Pet Foods.

The 1970s was an era of rapid growth in the advertising industry. Mainstream media was expanding with newspapers, magazines, radio and television attaining record levels of readership and audiences. New magazines such as *Cleo* were launched, and colour television was introduced in 1975. In this environment, advertisers were increasing their spending to reach potential buyers of their products and services. The big agencies such as Masius, George Patterson, John Clemenger, J Walter Thompson and Ogilvy & Mather were glamorous places to work and staff were well rewarded.

The research work at Masius included group discussions, later known as focus groups. It was a methodology that Bruce had never undertaken before, so it was a question of learning on the job – and hunting for people to participate in the groups. Friends and friends of friends were recruited. The focus group soon became an important element in most research programs, both market and social, and fortunately, the recruiting of respondents became more organised and professional!

Bruce and Sue went to London in 1972 and Bruce was able to get a research job with Masius there. Sue enlisted with a nursing agency and worked in several of the large London hospitals. While working in London Bruce met Peter Butler, a market researcher with Colgate-Palmolive, a huge Masius client. The relationship with Peter was to flourish over later decades when he migrated to Australia. Another acquaintanceship was made with John Wigzell, a market researcher working with another large advertising agency, Ogilvy & Mather, and this too had implications for the future. Bruce and Sue lived in the UK for two years and then went to South Africa. It was Bruce's work on the Colgate-Palmolive account that took them to their new destination. A small South African agency had won the account in that country and Masius was encouraged by Colgate and other international clients, such as Wilkinson Sword, to acquire the South African agency which then began to recruit a band of ex-pats from around the Masius global network to help service the international clients. Bruce was offered a position and he and Sue went to Pretoria, the nation's capital, where they stayed for a year. Largely because of the oppressive and inhumane apartheid system, they decided to return to Australia.

After their three years abroad, the couple returned to Melbourne and Bruce re-joined Masius working in account service instead of market research. The agency was about to join forces with a large American group, and it became

D'Arcy McManus Masius. Around this time, the Smiths discovered Sue was pregnant, and son Paul was born in 1976. Their daughter Georgia was born in 1981.

In 1975 Masius did the Liberal Party's advertising for the federal election held on December 13 of that year. The work proved divisive inside the agency – political advertising was an anathema to some of the agency people and it was a highly emotional time in the nation's history. This was the election that followed the unprecedented dismissal of the ALP government led by Gough Whitlam on November 11, 1975 by Governor-General Sir John Kerr. Whitlam's government had only been elected in 1972 and this was the most turbulent period in Australian politics since Federation. The 1975 double-dissolution election was won decisively by the Liberal-National Party coalition led by Malcolm Fraser. The chairman of Masius, Len Reason, became an authority on political advertising and wrote learned newspaper articles on the topic.

Late in his time at Masius, by complete co-incidence Bruce re-connected with Peter Butler whom he had met in London. Peter had migrated to Australia in 1977 after a brief stay in New Zealand. He had been appointed marketing manager for Beecham Group's consumer division. On his first day Peter received details of the suite of products he would be handling which included Enos Fruit Salts. He was then introduced by telephone to the Enos account executive at the advertising agency, which happened to be Bruce. There were to be several more encounters in the coming years.

Account service in a large advertising agency was never Bruce's preferred career choice. 'I hated working in account service. You were always compromising yourself, and for me the final straw was when I was asked to tell an outright lie to protect a colleague at the agency. I refused to do so and resigned soon after.' His time in account service convinced him that market research was his vocation.

In 1977 Bruce and another researcher Margot Weir opened their market research firm, Weir and Smith. Their client list was blue-chip and included several Masius advertising clients such as shaving products manufacturer

Wilkinson Sword, pharmaceutical and consumer goods company Beecham and the Australian Wool Corporation. They then attracted several new clients that were not part of the Masius stable such as the Department of Agriculture. With these clients, the new partnership had an outstanding first year.

Margot and Bruce first based their firm in a modest office, close to the landmark Prahran Market in Melbourne's inner south-east. The research landscape was changing due to societal changes – more women had entered the workforce and there was greater mobility and flexibility in workplaces. The old-style door-to-door field research was disappearing in favour of telephone and shopping mall surveys. The shopping mall was still a relatively new retail concept with the first in Victoria opening at Chadstone in Melbourne's east in 1960. The malls offered opportunities to rapidly survey a large cross-section of the community. Weir and Smith set up a mini-supermarket display in the Prahran Town Hall where they could test shelf facings and packaging ideas. Shoppers' reactions were readily measured and recorded.

Bruce and Margot moved their offices to Tasma Terrace, an historic three-storey terrace house complex in East Melbourne, on the fringe of the CBD. Soon after the move, Margot decided to relocate to Sydney, which ended the partnership. After the business relationship was terminated in 1980, Bruce found new, less expensive accommodation at Jolimont Terrace. This coincided with the formation of a new partnership, Smith & Sharp. Bruce had met Kevin Sharp through Weir and Smith's work with Telecom. Kevin had started there in 1972 in a clerical role and then worked in the marketing department where he developed a fascination with marketing and then research. When Telecom started what was believed to be the first market research unit in a government agency, he transferred and loved the work. To further his career, he gained a degree and was promoted to head of the market research unit. Telecom then decided that, as a promotion, Kevin should return to the marketing department. He decided he would leave Telecom rather than accept this move. He and Bruce decided to join forces and Smith & Sharp was formed as soon as Kevin departed Telecom.

Because of his extensive knowledge of the rapidly changing telecommunications field, Smith & Sharp attracted clients such as Australia Post and Ericsson Australia. For Australia Post, Smith & Sharp researched the marketing feasibility of an electronic messaging and mail delivery network based on facsimile machines. It was a huge project that entailed researching potential demand for an unknown service.

A highly innovative research project of the early 1980s involved seeking new ways to promote cricket in primary schools. The research was commissioned by the Australian Cricket Board (now Cricket Australia). The ACB was concerned about a decline in cricket participation rates among young (primary school age) children. The research established that there were three main barriers, and these were:

1. Domination by naturally talented children (predominantly boys) who monopolised games;
2. Fear of the hard cricket ball (especially for girls) and rejection of the then substitute tennis ball as a suitable alternative, and;
3. Domination of female teachers at primary school level who were not predisposed to cricket as a first option.

The task therefore was to design a new version of the game that would allow young girls and boys to play cricket without fear of being hurt by heavy wooden cricket bats and hard balls. Research had a key role by going into schools and playing a new form of the game, learning from observation and feedback and then tweaking the format. Eventually what emerged was called *Kanga Cricket*. The new game involved a softer but still solid plastic ball which removed the fear of being hurt; new rules whereby every player had an equal opportunity to bowl and bat (which addressed the talented kid domination and female intimidation factor) and finally a simplified set of rules. Light, easily portable plastic equipment was designed making it easier for teachers to quickly convene a game anywhere where there was space available and on any surface.

Kanga Cricket was launched in January 1984 by Prime Minister R J L (Bob) Hawke. In attendance were some of the nation's great current and past cricketers – Richie Benaud, Ian and Greg Chappell, Dennis Lillee and Kim Hughes. A former English fast bowler, Frank Tyson, who had migrated to Australia and become a cricket commentator was also there. Leading up to the launch, the Australian Cricket Board had sought sponsorships and it approached the Australian Dairy Corporation (ADC). The ADC saw this as an opportunity to promote dairy products to young consumers and agreed to be a sponsor. The funding ensured that all schools that wanted to participate were provided with the equipment. At the launch, the ADC's support was praised by Hawke.

The modified game became an immense, popular success and was later exported. It became *Kiwi Cricket* in New Zealand and was also adopted in England. The game is still widely played and has helped restore cricket to the position of highest participation sport in Australia.

For Bruce, it was another case of paths crossing as the ADC's marketing manager at that time was Peter Butler. He had joined in 1982 and was to work at the ADC until 1989 during which time he often retained the services of Smith & Sharp and then Sutherland Smith. The Australian Cricket Board also retained the services of the researchers for several years after the *Kanga Cricket* success.

Bruce and Kevin also undertook research for some of Victoria's most prestigious private schools, including Geelong Grammar, Christ Church Grammar and Marcellin College. This work was largely surveying parents of the schools' students to determine their expectations and satisfaction levels.

The Smith & Sharp partnership that had been formed in 1980 began to break up around 1983. It was not an acrimonious parting, the two partners simply had different interests and expertise. Kevin established his own firm and operated as a sole trader. This was a time when the Australian economy, because of international and local issues, was in deep recession. In 1982-83 national debt had risen to record levels, unemployment had reached 10.3 per cent, its highest post-war level, and a severe drought affected the nation's primary industries which were the major export earners in that era. The recession was seen by most political observers as a major factor in the downfall in March 1983 of Malcolm Fraser's coalition government. The Australian Labor Party led by Bob Hawke was swept into power.

Bruce recalled a period of six to nine months when no paid research work was undertaken. There were proposals totalling $100,000 outstanding but clients were reluctant to commission research in the prevailing economic environment. It was a challenging time for the Smith family as they had just moved into a newly purchased two-storey house in North Caulfield. Sue's part-time nursing work helped cover some of the living costs. Bruce took on two casual lecturing positions to provide additional funds. Both involved teaching market research; one at the Holmes Business College, a privately-owned facility in the city; the other was with the Chisholm Institute in Caulfield. The Holmes position was the less onerous as it involved a shorter lecture time, whereas at Chisholm he was expected to undertake a combined, back-to-back lecture and tutorial. It ran on Monday nights, from 6pm-10pm.

When the partnership was finally terminated, Bruce kept the Smith & Sharp business name but continued as a sole trader. 'I found it very lonely and unfulfilling. I even applied for some jobs with large corporations and industry associations at that time. My ambition had not diminished but there were huge self-doubts and considerable financial pressures.'

Throughout those years, Bruce had been actively involved with the Victorian division of the Market Research Society of Australia (MRSA), having joined in 1977. His involvement gave him a good understanding of the industry and its future. He knew that research was his vocation and, through the MRSA saw ample evidence that the sector was resilient and would continue to expand. In Australia market research was first undertaken in the late 1920s and it had grown strongly from then. Advertisers, media organisations and political parties all had an insatiable desire to learn more about their markets. The 1982-83 recession was no more than a temporary setback.

3

The Boy From Maitland

Allan Max Sutherland was born at Maitland in the Hunter Valley of New South Wales on December 1, 1944. Always known as Max, he is the youngest of three siblings with two older sisters, June and Delma. Maitland is a regional city of nearly 70,000 people, 32km north-west of Newcastle and around 165km north of Sydney. Maitland traces its history to colonial days when several convict settlements were established there around 1818. It is also the birthplace in 1894 of Herbert Vere (Bert) Evatt, war-time cabinet minister, leader of the ALP and judge. Legendary boxer Les Darcy was also born in Maitland in 1895.

Allan and Myrtle Sutherland, Max's parents, had met and married in Grafton, a regional town in the Northern Rivers region of NSW, close to the Queensland border. His father, known by the nickname of Joe,

The boy from Maitland

was a railway worker and in later years he also worked with Myrtle when they ran a corner store in Maitland.

Allan died of a stroke when Max was eight years old. His mother felt she could not work long hours and look after an eight-year-old child, so he was sent to a home for boys – the Woodlands boys' home in Wallsend, a suburb of Newcastle. Named after a coal mining town near Newcastle-on-Tyne in the UK, Wallsend was first settled in the 1850s. It is 32km from Maitland.

First opened in 1944 as a boys' and girls' home, Woodlands became a boys-only home a year later and a separate girls' home was established. The boys' home was closed in 1981 and gained considerable notoriety in 2013 when the Royal Commission into Institutional Responses to Child Sexual Abuse was told about a paedophile ring that operated at the home during the 1970s. Run by the United Protestant Association, Woodlands was converted to an aged care facility after its closure. Fortunately for Max and the boys who were there in the 1950s, they had no encounters with abuse. His memories of life at Woodlands are emotional and diverse. 'I have memories of feeling lonely, self-conscious and a little isolated while trying to fit in. I recall us sneaking across the fields to where there was an old mineshaft that was incredibly deep and filled with water. We used to go swimming in it. My early morning job was to milk one or two cows by hand so that we had milk for the breakfast table. My mother or one of my sisters would visit every second Saturday and we would go to the local movie theatre. When it came time for her to depart, it was always an emotionally wrenching time that is indelibly etched into my memory.'

He also recalls having to submit to the intensive religious commitments. 'Because it was the United Protestants boys' home, we had to spread ourselves around. All of us had to go to a different "brand" of church each Sunday morning followed back at Woodlands with Sunday School, and as if that wasn't enough, then scripture in the afternoon. Three sessions, a full day, of indoctrination for someone who, even earlier, at age four or five had taken a stand against going to church or Sunday School at all. It was hard to take and did nothing to endear me to religion.'

After 12 months at the home, Max's elder sister June who is 12 years his senior, generously offered to take Max into her home near Maitland for three weekdays a week even though she was newly married. Their mother was then able to take back Max for the other two weekdays and the weekend. After completing his primary education, he attended Maitland Boys' High School. While his results were reasonable, by the time he got to fourth year, he wanted to leave but his mother insisted that he stay. He rebelled by failing the year and his mother relented, allowing him to leave school but arranging for him to have an aptitude test to discover what his capabilities and what job he should pursue. 'They told me to be a linotype operator but there were no opportunities for me – fortunately. Linotype, which was part of an old-style printing technology, soon became obsolete.' Instead, Max found a job selling toys and hobbies in a retail store in Newcastle. He then moved to selling electrical appliances at various other retailers that sold televisions, washing machines and other domestic items.

Max was also a keen sportsman. As a schoolboy he swam competitively but gave it up for springboard diving and achieved second place in the NSW State Under-16 Schoolboy Championships. In later years he played competition squash but never at an elite level.

The life-changing event for Max was when he met Mel Enright in September 1965. He had backed, at very favourable odds, a horse called *Duo*, the winner of the Newcastle Gold Cup, so he and a friend were celebrating and were somewhat inebriated. They decided to gate-crash a local Miss Australia quest fund-raising ball at which Mel was one of the contestants. He met her there and managed to remember when they chanced to meet again a few weeks later at a Maitland harness racing 'trots' event. Their conversation at that event led to a promise to meet at the town hall dance the following Saturday. When he took her home from the dance, it was the beginning of a close, loving relationship. Within two weeks, they were secretly engaged and did not announce it for some months.

Mel was also born in Maitland, the fifth of seven children. Max was 21 and decided that if he and Mel were to marry and have a family, he needed to complete his education and pursue a career. He had tried night school before, but he was now motivated to make a third attempt. 'Attending five nights a week while working full time was the hardest thing I have ever done,' he said. He managed to pass his final year's secondary schooling and wanted to do a university degree but had little idea of what discipline. 'All I knew about was sales and the only thing that was close was called "marketing" and the only place that offered the course was the University of New South Wales in Sydney. So, in February 1967 Mel and I married in Maitland, and we then went to Sydney.'

When they first moved to Sydney, Max and Mel lived close to the university in Kensington, and then in Randwick and enjoyed exploring campus lifestyle. Later they moved to Scotland Island in Pittwater – an idyllic island environment that supported a small community with access only by ferry. Eric Anderson's – Max's electrical goods employer in Newcastle – had offered him a part-time job in its Sydney store. Mel urged him to enrol full-time and, if the combination of that and working part-time proved too onerous, she would support him. Max did enrol full-time and managed to work in the Barrack Street store in Sydney's CBD two or three days a week for the first year. He was then awarded a scholarship so ceased working in his second year. In his third year came another life changing event when he was employed part-time as a market research analyst with Coca-Cola. 'Coca-Cola was my introduction to on-the-job market research and a whole new world that valued intellectual ability and had generous salaries along with liberal expense accounts.' Mel, not to be left behind, also returned to study and in a marathon effort also completed the HSC (Higher School Certificate) at night school five nights a week and then completed an honours Arts degree majoring in political science at the University of NSW.

Max was invited to tutor at the university and he later became a lecturer there. This was to be the beginning of his career in academia. It was at the University of NSW where Max was forcibly exposed to an international perspective on marketing. His professor told Max in 1972 that he would be lecturing in international marketing the following year. Max replied, 'I've never been out of the country. I don't know anything about international marketing.' With sponsorship funds, the university arranged for Max and a colleague, Ross Cameron, to travel through South-East Asia for 10 weeks interviewing Australian businesspeople who worked in marketing in the region. They took back-pack video equipment – it was reel-to-reel monochrome – this was before the days of colour and their mission was to produce footage that could be used as lecture material to educate budding young marketing students in Australia.

In 1971, while still lecturing at the university, Max co-founded a market research company called Foresearch, the name being a combination of 'forecasting and research'. His partner and CEO was one of his former University of NSW students, Len Mannel. One of their first tasks was a groundbreaker. The Australian branch of a global pharmaceuticals company commissioned *Foresearch* to investigate why doctors were regularly prescribing the psychotropic drug Valium rather than alternative medications. Len ran a series of focus groups with general practitioners to find the answers. It was the first time in Australia that doctors had participated in focus groups. Held over dinner in a private room at a Travelodge hotel, the doctors were asked during the group sessions why they specifically prescribed Valium for patients exhibiting stress, anxiety, depression and related symptoms. Their immediate response was, 'Because it's so effective, it is so good.' After considerable discussion and a glass of wine as the evening progressed it emerged there was a widespread misconception amongst the GPs that Valium was a comparatively mild drug and was therefore relatively harmless. They also believed that two out of three patients would recover without any form of medication but given that patients expected their doctor to prescribe something, the GPs believed if they did not provide a prescription their patient would simply go to another doctor. Although they didn't consciously admit it to themselves, they were prescribing Valium largely for the placebo effect. Other similar medications were considered much stronger and hence were thought to pose greater health and self-harm risks for the patients.

It soon became apparent that other pharmaceutical companies were seeking similar answers for their products. Max and Len set up a syndicated focus group service, funded by them, where the findings of the focus groups were sold to multiple manufacturers.

Foresearch soon developed a reputation as a leader and innovator in pharmaceutical and farm chemicals research. But some 12 months after its launch, Mannel decided to leave for personal reasons and Max resigned from the university to run the business. He did this for a year or so before selling it to another pharmaceutical market research company for what he described as a pittance. He learned from the experience and *Foresearch* remained a reputable agency in the pharmaceuticals market until 2011 when it was acquired by a French multinational and merged into its research division.

While studying marketing, Max realised he had always had an interest in psychology and that marketing was a vicarious way of studying psychology. When exiting *Foresearch* in 1976, he managed to talk his way into the Sydney University master's degree course in psychology. The university was reluctant because he had not graduated in psychology in his undergraduate degree. It relented and he was delighted to find that in his class there were two other market researchers, Tony Wheeler and Warwick Hoare, who had formed the Sydney half of the market research company Yann Campbell Hoare Wheeler. While exiting Foresearch and studying for his master's, Max worked briefly with the Overseas Telecommunications Commission (OTC) which eventually became part of Telstra. OTC was a leader in international telecommunications technologies but had little in-house marketing expertise. Management's response was to hire a market researcher – Max. From 1977, OTC became a household brand with a television campaign aimed at European migrants who had left family members in their countries of origin. Called *Go home on the telephone* and accompanied by the iconic Barbara Streisand song, 'The Way We Were', the campaign was credited with generating record numbers of overseas telephone calls and won an international advertising award.

In 1977, an attractive job opportunity in academia led Max and Mel with their two young daughters to move to Melbourne. The girls were Keli, who was born in 1974, and Julia, born in 1976. While working at OTC Max was contacted by Barry Elliott, a market researcher with whom he had worked at Coca-Cola. Elliott was lecturing in Melbourne and was moving back to Sydney and into the advertising world. He asked Max whether he was interested in the lecturing position – and he was. As a result, Max was offered a senior lectureship at the Caulfield Institute of Technology (CIT). It was in 1977, with the restructuring of tertiary and vocational education, that CIT first offered degree courses. Further restructuring occurred in 1981 and CIT merged with Frankston State College to become Chisholm Institute, and in 1996 Chisholm became part of Monash University.

Although he had tenure, Max and Mel had planned to return to Sydney after three years. However, the family fell in love with Melbourne, so they never returned permanently. Max found Caulfield Institute an exciting place to work with its emphasis very much on teaching the practical rather than esoteric theory. Max's early research efforts there inspired his colleagues to a greater focus on research. These, together with the brilliant public relations talents of the then PR officer at CIT, Pete Steedman, began to generate regular, favourable national publicity for CIT's marketing department. Steedman, a former editor of university student newspapers, was a colourful and charismatic character who later briefly served as a Labor MP in Federal Parliament. After some 18 months of Steedman's and Max's efforts, Caulfield Institute of Technology became widely regarded as the best campus in Australia to study marketing. Max was happy at CIT, but he wanted more international experience, so he pitched an idea to his dean, John Miller. With Miller's support, Max advertised in an American marketing journal for an American professor to participate in an exchange of positions and residences for 12 months.

He received three replies one of which was from a professor at Kent State University in north-east Ohio some 80km from Chicago. A 12-month lectureship was subsequently arranged from mid-1979 at Kent State. Kent is a university town and its university gained national and international notoriety when, in 1970 students who were holding a protest rally against the Vietnam War were fired on by members of the Ohio National Guard. Four students, all aged between 19 and 20, were killed and nine wounded. Founded in 1910, the university survived this traumatic event and has, for most of its existence, been regarded as a top-tier American university.

Max swapped jobs and houses with the American professor and the Sutherland family moved to the United States. In his time there, Max completed his preliminary studies for a PhD in psychology and lectured in market research. While he lectured, Mel commenced a master's degree in education. At a marketing conference Max met a young assistant professor from the Wharton School, University of Pennsylvania. His name was John Rossiter and he was originally from Perth. A long personal, academic and business relationship followed.

When Max and Mel returned to Australia in 1980 Max researched and wrote his thesis which was completed in 1986. The year in Ohio was a life-changing experience for Max and Mel. Shortly after they returned, their son was born, and he was aptly named Kent. Years later they took Kent, who was by then a teenager, to see the university he was named after. He was impressed but wryly commented that he was so glad his father had not taken one of the other positions offered at Kalamazoo College!

Max recalls being spoilt with resources at Kent State. 'I was offered the services of a full-time research assistant. In Melbourne, I had raised $5000 from *The Age* newspaper to fund a part-time research assistant but what would I do with a full-time research assistant? I was told the assistant could mark my test papers for me, as well as help with my research and do other tasks. As I was there for only 12 months, I could not see myself using a full-time person, so I opted to share my research assistant with another lecturer. The experience made me realise just how under-resourced most Australian universities were by comparison.'

When they returned to Melbourne, Max resumed lecturing at Caulfield Institute, but it was to be a relatively short stay. He quickly became frustrated with the lack of resources – there was even a restriction on photocopying. If he stayed, he would have had to perform burdensome administrative roles as there was no help from any research assistant. Max resigned after a year and joined the major research agency, McNair Anderson, a pioneering firm that traced its history in Australia to the early 1930s. It was an agency that became synonymous with radio and television ratings and was at the time the largest market research firm in Australia. It also conducted political opinion polling as well as standard market research. Max stayed for around 12 months, but he found he was not well suited to working in large organisations. He considered returning to academia but after a discussion with Mel decided to set up as a sole trader and work from home. A M Sutherland & Associates was set up, and from the outset there was ample work coming his way. It was a telephone call from a business friend and researcher Geoff Alford that made him aware of spare office space available at Jolimont Terrace and this brought Max into regular contact with Bruce. Alford had also worked at Tasma Terrace where Bruce and Margot Weir had briefly been located.

Soon after moving to the new office, Max learned from Kevin Sharp that the Smith & Sharp partnership was breaking up. Meanwhile, Max had established a business affiliation with another of his former Sydney students, Martin Van Herk of Stochastic Marketing, and they were thriving on the newly minted continuous tracking research. It was very early days for continuous tracking, but its potential was exciting.

Van Herk was also the major shareholder of Nationwide Research Services, a business that provided field work services to other research companies. Field work in those days comprised interviews done over the telephone, in shopping malls and elsewhere. Interviewers were hired on a casual basis and they worked throughout the nation. The data collected would then be collated and presented as tables to the research firms by Nationwide. Smith & Sharp and others would subcontract their field work to firms like Nationwide.

Van Herk was acknowledged by Max and many others as being quite brilliant but he parted company with Nationwide and Sutherland Smith after becoming enmeshed in several legal issues that some years later led to the Australian Securities Commission (later known as the Australian Securities and Investments Commission or ASIC) banning him as a company director for two and a half years.[1]

Nationwide continued to provide field work to many market research firms. It too was briefly located at Jolimont Terrace, next door to where Bruce, Max and the other researchers worked. Bruce and Max maintained a close working relationship with Nationwide and eventually acquired a major shareholding in the business because interviewing had become such a critical part of their continuous tracking research.

The move to Jolimont Terrace in 1983 into the same building as Bruce was a fortuitous event. It seeded a growing relationship that eventually culminated in the creation of the entity Sutherland Smith.

4

The De Facto Partnership

When Bruce and Max first decided in 1983 that they would work together, they formed what they called a 'de facto' partnership. It was a prudent agreement that created a solid foundation for their long-term success. The failure of Bruce's two previous partnerships and the debt his business was carrying was only part of the reason for their innovative arrangement. They were both aware that partnerships in many different business sectors had high failure rates.

In May 1986 they moved from Jolimont Terrace to rented offices in Maple Close Business Park, an office complex on Church Street, Richmond close to the banks of the Yarra River. There they started what was to become a highly successful business enterprise. Another researcher from Jolimont Terrace, Keith Patterson, had found the Church Street premises and had intended to share some of the office accommodation but fate intervened, and he relocated to Perth leaving Bruce and Max with a little more space, and rental cost, than they had anticipated. It was a financial hurdle that soon proved to be a bonus and one they were able to overcome with the rapid expansion of their services.

The de facto partnership involved operating as two separate financial entities but presenting to clients and all external markets as one business until they were satisfied that they could work successfully together. They had registered the Sutherland Smith name in April 1983 while still at Jolimont Terrace, so Max called his business Sutherland Smith Continuous Tracking and Bruce named his Sutherland Smith Qualitative Input. They chose these names because of the differences in their disciplines — Max focussing on quantitative research and Bruce's work being mainly qualitative.

Why Sutherland Smith rather than Smith Sutherland? According to Bruce; 'Sutherland Smith rolled off the tongue much better than Smith Sutherland!' It was that simple.

They shared resources including their offices and support staff. They even experimented with commercialising their secretarial services registering Fax 'N Figures as a business entity which could provide typing, copying and printing services to clients who faxed in their handwritten copy. The rapid growth of the Sutherland Smith business however soon curtailed this venture which then became the dedicated office service hub within the company.

To encourage openness and trust, they never closed their office doors and readily shared their knowledge and experience. The openness permeated their business and staff were rarely if ever reticent about discussing any work-related issues.

'I had spoken to Kevin Sharp and was impressed by him telling me that the dissolution of the Smith & Sharp partnership was amicable,' Max recalled. 'He told me that Bruce was a really good partner and an honest and transparent person, but I felt the need to be really cautious.' Max's unfortunate experience with a number of previous business associates was also a reason for his caution.

Structuring the de facto partnership was done by an accountant who had been Max's accountant before taking on the Sutherland Smith role. Max had been referred to him by a lawyer who Max had met while lecturing at the Caulfield Institute. In addition to setting up the de facto partnership, the accountant helped Bruce resolve his financial difficulties arising from the previous

THE DE FACTO PARTNERSHIP

partnerships. He soon joined the board and became known as 'the third director'. Both Bruce and Max agree that his role was pivotal in the success of the de facto partnership and the long-term success of Sutherland Smith. He has chosen to remain anonymous for the publishing of this book.

The Prince Alfred Hotel at 619 Church Street Richmond which was built around 1899, is listed by the Heritage Council of Victoria and described as, '...historically, socially, architecturally and aesthetically significant to the locality of Richmond...' Across the road from the Sutherland Smith offices at Maple Close, the old pub also became significant to the partnership's success.

The historic Prince Alfred Hotel where Max and Bruce resolved issues at their 'decision table'.

From the time Max and Bruce moved into their new abode, the hotel became a place where they would go to resolve any differences or difficult issues. They would sit at what they called 'the decision table', order lunch or drinks, and discuss whatever concerns they had. These included hiring new staff, financial matters and potential conflicts of interest. The decision table was in a small alcove, so it offered some privacy and the publican was happy to reserve it for two of his regular patrons. Bruce and Max would sit at the table at least once a week and often more frequently. Most discussions that they can recall ended with a positive outcome —

Revisiting the 'decision table' in later years.

disputes were resolved, agreements reached on future directions, who to employ and many other aspects of their business activities were aired.

From the outset, the partners agreed that they would not work for any tobacco companies and nor would they conduct political research. On the latter topic, Bruce had seen how divisive political advertising had been during his time at Masius and he did not want to see a similar situation occur at Sutherland Smith.

The de facto partnership was harmonious and productive and so, after a relatively short period of time, the two de facto partners agreed that it was time to formalise the arrangement. As a result, Sutherland Smith became far more than just a registered business name, it was their corporate entity. They had established trust in each other, and Bruce's debts had, with their accountant's professional assistance, been brought under control. The momentum the two partners had created in that de facto period continued. They were both equally committed to continuous tracking which was gaining increasing acceptance by large, national and international brands, and companies such as Gillette, Unilever, Beecham, Rosella, Tooheys, Swan and XXXX beers, Murray Goulburn, the Australian Dairy Corporation and others. It was not only tracking the effectiveness of their advertising, the research data was also able to track changes in consumer behaviour, competitor activity and the impact of external events.

With the growth came a need to employ more people and, in the second half of the 1980s, several key appointments were made. Most of these appointments were made with the total commitment of Bruce and Max so they were only confirmed after discussions at the Prince Alfred's decision table.

Stephen Prendergast joined the firm in mid-1987. A scientist by training, Stephen transitioned from industrial chemistry to marketing when he joined the accounting and management consulting firm Peat Marwick (soon to become part of the global firm, KPMG). A junior consultant in the Peat Marwick marketing department, Stephen was also studying at Chisholm Institute where one of his lecturers was Bruce Smith. Bruce had originally commenced his lecturing career because of his family's financial difficulties during the recession of 1982-83. He stayed on at Chisholm and in later years recalled: 'Having come into market research at a time when there was no formal teaching of it and where one "learned-on-the-job" I actually found the lecturing helped me with my work. It provided a much-needed theoretical context plus a more detailed understanding of various techniques and methodologies.'

Originally appointed as a support for Bruce, Stephen proved to be one of the key appointments that helped generate the Sutherland Smith growth path during this key period. His original role was qualitative research in the investor relations field, and he recalls interviewing stockbrokers, analysts and others. It was a few months before the stockmarket crash of mid-October and the investor relations work soon dried up as a result of the massive downturn.

Fortunately, around this time the continuous tracking work was growing, and Stephen quickly transitioned into the discipline. His recollection of the developing field: 'The way it worked in those days, the people working on the tracking studies did a lot of the "top to bottom" work themselves. They liaised with the field operation, tweaked questionnaires, analysed the data, produced time-series plots, were rudimentary plotters who grabbed pens and traced time-series lines, stuck on acetate to present results and did own analysis.'

Another important appointment around the same time as Stephen was Angus Kinnaird. Also in 1987, Peggy Duell joined – first in a part-time role and then as a full-timer. She was to stay for 18 years and her story is told in Chapter 14.

Omnia Holland joined Sutherland Smith in September 1988. She was one of the first senior appointments made by Max and Bruce and she was to play a major role in the company for a decade. Omnia had completed a double degree in Psychology – clinical and research design/statistics – and then a postgraduate thesis in Applied Social Psychology. Omnia then practised as a clinical psychologist for two years before joining McNair Anderson. She discovered she disliked psychological practice and that market research appealed. Her qualifications and training gave her the skills for both quantitative and qualitative research. She worked in the firm's Melbourne office for around two years. It was a time when McNair Anderson was swallowed up in mergers and acquisitions. Through a merger it had become AGB McNair. AGB was a UK-based, global firm and it acquired 60 per cent of the Australian company. Under the new management there was a restructure – Omnia's role diminished, and she became disenchanted. She resigned and took a research position with the Road Traffic Authority (later known as VicRoads). There she headed a multi-disciplined unit that developed state government policy. A key part of Omnia's role was researching the political impact of any policy changes or innovations. She was about to move to the Gas & Fuel Corporation, another statutory authority when an alternative job offer appeared – it came, via Malcolm Cameron, a recruitment consultant retained by Bruce and Max. She was initially interviewed by Bruce and the role he was offering appealed to Omnia – he spoke of innovation and creativity, thinking of new and better ways of doing research. After the regimented methodologies of state government, Omnia was excited by the prospects and, after a separate meeting with Max, she accepted.

From Bruce's standpoint, Omnia proved to be a key appointment. As she was one of the first senior people to join the firm, Bruce and Max only agreed on her appointment after an extended session at the decision table. Her appointment freed Bruce from being the principal qualitative researcher and enabled him to focus more of his time and energy on the development of continuous tracking which was soon to become an international business.

Omnia grew the qualitative research portfolio and renamed it *Custom Design*. Several major new clients were won, and these included the global pharmaceuticals manufacturer GlaxoSmith Kline, Kraft Foods, the ANZ bank, Myer department stores and lotteries and gaming giant Tattersalls. Several of these accessed both qualitative and quantitative services. Omnia proved to be remarkably successful at attracting new business to the firm.

The year that Omnia joined – 1988 – proved to be a pivotal one in the history of Sutherland Smith. The brand MarketMind Technologies was first registered in Australia and a Sutherland Smith office in Sydney was opened.

5

THE CONTINOUS TRACKING EVOLUTION

The concept of continuous tracking had evolved from the beginning of the 1980s. It was a demand driven evolution – companies in the highly competitive consumer goods and services marketplace wanted more timely, rapid response quantitative research. Their environments were rapidly changing in an era of global transformation. Automation of production lines, the beginning of computerisation of workplaces and larger and more rapid transport modes all contributed to the transformation. In 1982, *Time* magazine named 'the computer' as its 'person of the year' – the first time it was not a real person. It was an acknowledgement of the impact computerisation was about to make on humankind. Two years later Apple introduced the Macintosh, a highly advanced and user-friendly personal computer that had immense appeal. The information technology revolution was well underway, even though it would be some years before the internet's arrival and proliferation.

Point-in-time research was becoming increasingly exposed as outdated and irrelevant because of its inability to accurately measure trends in a rapidly changing marketplace. The marketplace of six weeks ago, let alone six months, was no longer an adequate measure of the environment. The search for timelier and therefore more relevant market intelligence had begun.

Max had first encountered continuous tracking when he formed his alliance with Martin Van Herk. Van Herk had been a student of Max's at the University of NSW and was then research manager at Unilever in Australia. Founded in northern England in the 1890s, Unilever had grown into a global giant that manufactured and marketed a myriad of grocery and related brands. Unilever's growth was driven by its innovations in products and marketing. In 1962 it had spawned its own research firm in the UK which expanded into several European markets before being sold to the Ogilvy & Mather advertising group in 1986. New approaches to market research were always on the Unilever agenda and one of the developments it had begun to explore was how to do continuous tracking at reasonable cost. Van Herk left Unilever to set up his own company, Stochastic Marketing, and it would perform continuous tracking for Unilever and other businesses in Australia.

However, the concept had much earlier exposure. An article in the May-June 1968 edition of prestigious journal, the *Harvard Business Review*, entitled 'Monitor your market continuously', floated the idea of what was to become continuous tracking many years later. Co-authored by advertising executive Russell I Haley and an academic from the City University of New York, Ronald Gatty, the authors argued that large, 'one shot' studies failed to account for seasonal changes that impacted on consumer purchasing patterns. Their research found that even the sales of products which were unaffected by weather changes, such as watches, were impacted by seasonal factors, and that the types of consumers making the purchases varied according to the time of year. The authors made an accurate forecast: 'In short, we predict that the one-shot benchmark studies so common today will be replaced by a system of continuous research in which marketing research data are accumulated during every month of the year and summarized periodically.' It was remarkable foresight at a time when the most sophisticated equipment to be found in most offices were electric typewriters and telex machines.[2]

From the early 1980s, Max readily appreciated the challenges and often used the article to promote the cause. Max described it this way:

> With point-in-time research it was like taking a single frame from a movie and trying to interpret what was happening in the entire movie. It was obvious that tracking continuously would be better than snapshot research. The challenge was to find an economic method of doing it. Doing full-scale survey research every week was prohibitively expensive. Martin, building on his experience at Unilever, introduced ways of doing it economically – using smaller samples. However, surveying 50 to 100 people a week was not statistically significant – but it could be done by rolling weeks together to create a moving average. Over four weeks there would be a sample of 200 to 400 people and this was getting up towards statistical significance. In the UK a new company, Millward-Brown, had appeared on the scene using a similar concept. Martin, like Millward-Brown, emphasised graphing the output at a time when most research was presented as figures in tables. The graphs, however, had to be drawn up and plotted laboriously by hand because computer graphing had yet to appear. One of Martin's strengths was emphasising interpretation and recommendations – what the data means rather than just presenting it.

Max was at first sceptical, as a good academic should be, of this small sample research but he was progressively convinced it was a methodological breakthrough that despite the small samples, worked! Impressed by Van Herk's vision, A M Sutherland & Associates became the Victorian affiliate for Stochastic Marketing. The relationship lasted around two years but Max's commitment to continuous tracking was entrenched for the rest of his career.

The transition from Stochastic Marketing to Sutherland Smith Continuous Tracking involved an agreed, short-term licence fee to Van Herk.

THE CONTINUOUS TRACKING EVOLUTION

When Max and Bruce decided to make continuous tracking one of the core offerings of their partnership, the greatest challenge was to find ways to handle the masses of data – to enable instant accessing of that data and allow instant graphing and instant overlaying of series. All this was in pursuit of 'analytical speed' to be able to 'close in' on *causes*.

The information technology era was arriving and Max's interest in IT was about to pay off. The next few years were consumed by the pursuit to remove the labour intensity – to identify and develop the technology that would give Sutherland Smith a dynamic competitive advantage in the delivery of economic and affordable tracking analysis.

Also important in their competitive advantage was the overriding emphasis on going beyond data to tease out what the data meant in terms of action recommendations. Max gives credit to Ian Jackson, Marketing Director of Gillette Australia and one of their first clients for his focus on this. As Max told it:

> It was my very first graphical presentation to Gillette, and they were testing us out. After probably an hour of presenting the information, I thought I had done a pretty good job. But when I finished, Ian leaned back in his chair, folded his hands behind his head and said 'Max, what does all that *mean*?' That knocked my socks off. He didn't say it in a nasty way and I quickly realised the sheer amount of information was a bit overwhelming and he was genuinely asking for me to summarise my conclusions – what I would do based on that data? I was a bit unnerved trying to improvise but from that day on, I changed my style and the presentation style of our staff for all our clients. Our analysts were instructed to always lead with the conclusions and then proceed to provide the graphical and other evidence for those conclusions, not the other way around, as was customary in market research in those days. It was hard to do but

it worked well. Not the least because it made analysts focus on the conclusions and not get lost in mountains of data. If they had no conclusions, it meant they had nothing to say, so why were they there? It enforced a kind of quality control for Sutherland Smith and along with that came a competitive advantage that was barely visible to competitors.

Ian Jackson, who joined Gillette as a brand manager in 1979, first met Max in the early 1980s, before the days of Sutherland Smith. Ian spent over 20 years with Gillette and held several senior management positions in Australia and overseas. Ian was impressed by Max's independence and integrity. The combination of academic and commercial experience certainly appealed.

Continuous tracking was not unique to Sutherland Smith. During the 1980s, Sutherland Smith Continuous Tracking (SSCT), later to be called MarketMind, had Millward-Brown as its main competitor in Australia. Millward-Brown had introduced a form of continuous tracking in the UK in the late 1970s and progressively rolled it out in several countries including Australia where it subsequently acquired the highly successful and well-established market research company Yann Campbell Hoare Wheeler.

Sutherland Smith Continuous Tracking was, nevertheless, quickly becoming superior in many aspects. As the technology evolved, clients were provided with near real-time data which was enhanced with information about all the activity that took place in their marketplaces. The emphasis on what the data meant, in terms of what the client should do, was paramount. Sutherland Smith people would receive the data and then spend time intensively examining and assessing its relevance to the client. By being able to look beyond the obvious conclusions and assess societal, economic and other critical issues, the Sutherland Smith service presented a far more nuanced approach than its competitors.

As Bruce recalled:

> Our clients were given a highly interactive presentation. It was never just a 'data dump'. There was a front end and a back end. The front end was an engine of data storage, handling and interpretation. The rear end was the interactive presentation which enabled clients to interrogate the material and interrogate our interpretation of it. A significant feature of our product was the questionnaire. It wasn't just a series of questions; it was structured in modules which related to each other and they were often mathematically designed. One critical measure was what we called 'attitude share', and it was derived from perceptions of, and attitudes towards a brand. It determined what share of market a brand should be getting based on what was happening inside people's heads. The attitude share was measured on a scale. We attached weights to the responses and could therefore tell a client that its attitude share was, say 44 per cent but its actual market share was 38 per cent. How was this happening? Was a competitor's advertising more effective? Was point-of-sale the problem because the competitor was offering better deals? What about distribution – was the entire market being supplied or were there gaps? But arguably the main distinguishing feature of the early years of SSCT was the focus on interpreting the data and presenting clients with what we thought what was going on, what we thought was working, what wasn't and why. This was a tricky position to occupy since we were frequently telling highly paid professional executives things they may not have wanted to hear. This was ever so obvious when we were evaluating advertising campaigns, when our analysis became so precise, we could identify major weaknesses in advertising campaigns. This did not endear us to advertising agencies, some of which chose to

undermine our findings and alienate us from their clients rather than embrace the new-found knowledge. This had the effect of making us extremely careful about what we said and how we said it, and one way of achieving this was by what Max termed the presentation 'dry run', where the Sutherland Smith executive who was presenting the findings was required to make a full presentation to either of us at least one day out from the client presentation. This had many advantages: it enabled us to achieve a minimum standard of presentation, a consistent method of presenting and a great way of imparting our knowledge and skills to more junior staff.

One of the biggest impacts from these presentations was at McCain Foods where it became apparent that the sales and marketing departments operated on different wave lengths. It was clear that there were problems and the two departments were forced to come together. There were other companies with similar failings which were exposed by continuous tracking.

One of the early users of continuous tracking was the dairy giant, Murray Goulburn. A dairy farmers' co-operative that was established in 1950, Murray Goulburn was the manufacturer and marketer of several high-profile brands such as Devondale. In 1986 the company retained Sutherland Smith to undertake continuous tracking of its Devondale butter and track the launch of Devondale Dairy Soft. The former was a traditional butter while the latter was a blend of butter, canola oil and other products. Dairy Soft had been introduced in response to health concerns about the fat content of traditional butters. The continuous tracking soon established that Murray Goulburn's television commercials for the two products were creating confusion in the marketplace. Interviewed in the first edition of the newsletter, *Sutherland Smith Monitor*, Murray Goulburn's General Manager, Marketing & Sales, John Howell, praised the continuous tracking saying, 'It gave us a diagnostic tool for establishing a strategy for future commercial production so that we could avoid this confusion... We believe that it (continuous tracking) allows you to understand the way in which your communication is affecting customers' knowledge of your product and their claimed purchasing behaviour.' He vowed that his company would continue to use the service. The imprimatur of a major organisation such as Murray Goulburn was a significant fillip for the embryonic continuous tracking service which was still evolving.

Another early user of continuous tracking was the Australian Dairy Corporation and it was Peter Butler who retained Sutherland Smith from 1985. The ADC's charter was to promote the dairy industry, and this included manufactured dairy products such as butter, cheese and cream.

The first edition of the SS Monitor. Only around half a dozen editions were published.

The first of two major research projects conducted by Sutherland Smith in 1985 was a usage, consumption and awareness study on the market for cheese. The ADC had launched a major generic advertising and promotional program for Australian cheese, based on the slogan, 'Where's the cheese?' The celebrity chef, author and graphic artist, Peter Russell-Clarke was the presenter. The purpose of the research was to demonstrate to dairy farmers the effectiveness of the ADC's generic advertising and promotional activities. The second project commenced in 1988, when the industry was undergoing significant restructuring and the purpose and effectiveness of the ADC's role as well as diary farmer's funding of generic advertising and promotional campaigns was being questioned. While the research showed that the campaigns were successful, the industry had begun to scale down funding for the ADC in general and promotional programs specifically.

While the dairy industry was scaling down its promotional activities, the career of Peter Russell-Clarke soared into the stratosphere. He had his own cooking show called *Come and get it* on ABC television, was the presenter of advertisements for cheeses and other foods and authored several cookery books.

The growth of continuous tracking created the need for another two continuous tracking appointments in the late 1980s – Angus Kinnaird and Elick Teitelbaum. Angus and Elick were known to each other before they came to Sutherland Smith – they had worked together at Roy Morgan Research. Elick joined in late 1988 as a research analyst.

The growing success of the continuous tracking service made a positive impact on the Sutherland Smith business and it soon accounted for more than half of total revenue and profit. But handling the mass of data it generated remained too cumbersome and beyond the capability of existing IT (known as 'data processing' at the time) to provide interactivity. Max and Bruce wasted a lot of money on consultants who promised they could develop appropriate software. It proved beyond them. Max and Bruce struggled for a solution. The only option left was to try to develop the necessary software themselves in-house.

Neil Francis (left) and Kingsley Winikoff

The first element of finding the solution was the hiring of Kingsley Winikoff. Kingsley had worked at IBM in Australia and Israel during the 1960s and had several other pioneering roles before joining Sutherland Smith in 1989. He had briefly worked in IT at Australia's largest company, BHP before being recruited.

The next stage of impetus came from the development of the in-house IT tools. Programming specialists Dale Chant and Roland Seidel were employed at the beginning of the 1990s and they worked with Kingsley as their mentor. This change in approach proved to be the major turning point in the continuous tracking history and is detailed in Chapter 12. The two key initial programming developments were named Wintrak and G-tab. With these, SSCT had a clear competitive edge over rivals and this would prove a major advantage when it went global from the early 1990s. In simple terms, Wintrak and G-tab made MarketMind 'user friendly'. Wintrak was a graphics program and G-tab placed the database in the hands of the client. The client could interrogate the data without requiring the support of a data programmer or other IT specialist. The demographic profile, gender, shopping habits or other characteristics of consumers could be drawn from the data as needed. This information could often be extracted in no more than 20 seconds. Previously it would have taken two to four weeks turnaround time to answer a client's query. The process required that the query be referred from the researcher to the IT department and be slotted into their already busy schedules for processing.

A momentous though deceptively simple development in the program was the easy ability to show 'events' on the graphs such as out-of-stock times, sales promotion dates, price changes, pack changes and many others. These were stored in a file named the Events File and they could be searched and overlayed on any graph at any time in seconds. It was a simple but highly effective means of storing and identifying key local and international events, economic factors, promotional campaigns or competitor activity which could affect the performance of the brand or service being tracked. At client presentations, these could be instantly retrieved and displayed where performance had moved in unexplained way(s), and could be flagged on sales charts or other graphs. The event file represented a significant improvement in the MarketMind product and a major point of difference from major competitor Millward-Brown through its ability to demonstrate to clients how factors other than the most obvious ones of price and advertising, could affect brand performance.

From the beginning of 1994, when MarketMind was undertaking continuous tracking for the Australian Tourist Commission (later known as Tourism Australia), there were spikes in incoming tourists that were linked to events such as Sydney's Gay and Lesbian Mardi Gras which, from the early 1990s was attracting interstate and overseas visitors in growing numbers. At the launch of another new global advertising campaign, there was a spike in incoming tourists that was at first thought to be the result of the newly launched campaign. However, further analysis revealed that Australia's increased market share of tourists was accompanied by a corresponding decrease in tourists visiting Japan. Why was this so? Overlaying the Events File chronicled that there had been a major earthquake in Japan just before the lift in Australia's visitor numbers. While it was tempting to believe the spike was caused by Australia's newly released global campaign, the analysis showed it was not primarily the advertising campaign. Rather, international tourists originally intending to visit Japan, were understandably affected by publicity surrounding the earthquake and many switched to alternative holiday destinations, one of which was Australia. The Events File served to record and remind everybody of key events like this that could impact markets but might otherwise be overlooked. The Events File was not only a corporate memory, it also provided a market history.

MarketMind's competitive advantages required careful and detailed protection under intellectual property (IP) laws. Software, such as Wintrak had been developed and was unique to Sutherland Smith. Neil Francis, who joined the MarketMind team in 1995 recalls that training manuals had to carry watermarks on every page to deter photocopying or scanning. Neil also created a tagline for MarketMind which was, *Continuous interactive intelligence*. It reflected a growing trend amongst corporations to gather, analyse and interpret for themselves intelligence that impacted their businesses.

In later years many of the client-friendly features that were unique to MarketMind would be taken for granted as the IT revolution permeated the market-research industry and all aspects of the business world. In the 1980s and first half of the 1990s, they provided Sutherland Smith Continuous Tracking and then MarketMind with a significant competitive advantage.

A survey of continuous tracking clients, and ex-clients, was commissioned in mid-1990. The purpose of the survey was to determine how clients were using the information provided by Sutherland Smith and how the service could be improved. The findings were to be revealed at an internal seminar for all continuous tracking staff. The task was undertaken by Peter Wigney who was a lecturer at Chisholm Institute of Technology (later Monash University's Caulfield Campus), secretary of the Victorian division of the Market Research Society of Australia and had been marketing research manager at Dulux Australia. He interviewed 10 current and four past clients. In his summary Wigney observed: 'Quite a number of interviewees had a favourable reaction to the idea that Sutherland Smith were researching themselves.'

The findings were generally favourable, but the most commonly expressed concern was the cost of the service. Another aspect that was criticised by several respondents was the complexity of the graphic presentations which were done with overhead transparencies – there was no PowerPoint in those days. There was also some gentle criticism of the jargon used in presentations and other minor issues. The most strident criticism came from Bond Brewing alerting that this account was over-stretched. Appropriate action was taken recognising that Bond was not just one account; it had a different market in each state and needed more strategic input and personnel support at a state level, particularly in NSW and Queensland. Overall the survey found the clients readily saw the benefits of continuous tracking and were committed to the product. Furthermore, the survey was of great value to Bruce and Max since it focussed their attention on the features of the product that were most valued by clients. It led to immediate changes in how results were presented and provided even more incentive to develop a better method of graphical presentation.

6

Reforms of The 1980s

While the information technology revolution had commenced in the early 1980s, there were other major reformation programs taking place in Australia and other parts of the world. These were economic and social reforms that would have long-term impacts on all aspects of business, including market research.

The election in March 1983 of an ALP government led by Bob Hawke heralded a major reform and deregulation program of the Australian financial sector. Most of the reforms were driven by then-Treasurer Paul Keating and commenced with the exchange rate being floated in December 1983. This was followed by the deregulation of the banking and securities (stocks and shares) industries. The deregulation of the banking sector from the mid-1980s allowed foreign banks to gain licences in Australia and for new banks to emerge from building societies and other financial institutions. Australian markets that had been sheltered from competition were now part of the global marketplace.

One of the new banks, based in Sydney, was the Advance Bank and it became a Sutherland Smith client. Formed in 1985, it had previously been the NSW Permanent Building & Investment Society.

Another significant reform was enacted on 1 April 1987. Six independent, state-based stock exchanges were merged into the newly formed Australian Stock Exchange (ASX). A national and international share trading environment emerged. The new, highly competitive market meant that all listed companies and companies planning to float on the ASX needed to have a much deeper understanding of investors' expectations and behaviours. Shareholders and potential shareholders were operating in a more complex, rapidly changing environment.

This was also the era of the high-flying, maverick entrepreneurs such as Alan Bond, Robert Holmes à Court, Laurie Connell and Christopher Skase. Their emergence was largely due to the deregulated banking sector which provided them with easy access to large amounts of money. They fuelled volatility and uncertainty in financial markets – and most eventually crashed to earth with massive debts.

The multitude of reforms led to the emergence of investor relations as a new area of quantitative and qualitative research. Companies that were listed on the ASX, or those planning to list began to understand the importance of how they were perceived by investors and potential investors. It was not long before Sutherland Smith emerged as a leader in the field conducting

Eminent lawyer John Dahlsen's interview in the SS Monitor.

qualitative investor relations studies and quantitative shareholder surveys. To handle this work, a dedicated unit known as the Shareholder and Investor Relations Unit was established and headed by Bruce. The team varied according to needs, but key members included Stephen Prendergast, Omnia Holland and Mark Solonsch.

Their introduction to the field came via a prominent Melbourne lawyer and company director John Dahlsen. He was a partner in the law firm Corrs Pavey Whiting & Byrne (now Corrs Chambers Westgarth) and, over several years, his firm had advised Sutherland Smith on international licence agreements, employment contracts and confidentiality matters relating to the continuous tracking business. Bruce and Max had concerns that a rogue licensee or employee could steal the intellectual property and profit from it. Seeking advice from a top-tier law firm was a prudent move and, in return, it also generated a significant amount of investor relations work.

During the 1980s, Dahlsen was a non-executive director of several major companies including the Herald & Weekly Times (HWT), retail giant Myer and the ANZ bank. He also provided legal advice to companies that were contemplating, or engaged in, mergers and acquisitions. Dahlsen retained Sutherland Smith to undertake investor relations research into several large takeover battles that characterised the corporate world during this era.

In 1983, Myer entered a bidding war for Grace Brothers, a department store competitor. Dahlsen was deputy-chairman of Myer and it won the complex and drawn-out battle against opposition bids, including Westfield, FAI Insurance and Bond Corporation.

Dahlsen was chairman of the HWT when it became a takeover target from 1986. Rupert Murdoch's News Corporation launched a bid and there were competitive bids that came from Robert Holmes à Court's Bell Corporation, rival media group John Fairfax Ltd and corporate raider IEL. Eventually the Murdoch bid succeeded and Dahlsen stepped down as chairman.

The biggest and best-known takeover battle of the 1980s was the Robert Holmes à Court 1983-86 attempt to acquire what was then Australia's biggest company, BHP. His company, Bell Resources, managed to acquire around 30 per cent of BHP's shares before the defence strategy supported by another corporate giant, Elders IXL, and the 1987 stockmarket crash finally scuttled the bid. Dahlsen was a legal advisor to BHP and he commissioned Sutherland Smith to undertake research designed to monitor investor sentiment and responses to the bids by Holmes à Court.

In most of these battles, Sutherland Smith would do quantitative and qualitative research to ascertain the attitudes of ordinary shareholders and major market influencers such as stockbrokers, institutional investors and market analysts. The research would help Dahlsen and his boards and clients determine how best to develop strategies and to communicate with investors in bids and defences. There was also the critical issue of gaining the best outcome for all shareholders, large and small. Quoted in the first edition of *Sutherland Smith Monitor*, Dahlsen said shareholder research could add huge sums to shareholder funds.

Another company that retained Sutherland Smith for investor relations research was Mayne Nickless. The research was undertaken in 1987 and 1988 and it showed the company had improved its standing with professional investors through proactive communications. In 1987 it was viewed as, '...uninspiring, introverted, impersonal'. Improved earnings also enhanced the company's 1988 standing within the freight transport and logistics sector, moving it from third to second against Brambles, the sector leader, and TNT.[3]

Because of the highly confidential nature of this work, the activities of the Shareholder and Investor Relations Research Unit were rarely publicised or promoted. Strict corporation and stock exchange laws and regulations determined what, when and how information could be released.

7

SUTHERLAND SMITH – AND RINGHAM

In 1988, there was another Sutherland Smith landmark – the opening of an office in Sydney. At the time, Sydney was perceived as the corporate capital of Australia as there were more large companies headquartered there than in Melbourne or any other Australian city. There were several new or existing clients based in Sydney, and Max and Bruce felt these clients which included Bond Brewing, New South Wales Dairy Corporation and the Advance Bank, were best serviced from a Sydney office. The Bond Brewing business was national, but its brands operated independently in state markets. Beer brands had traditionally been based in states and their acquisition by national and international conglomerates did little to change state-based loyalties of consumers. The NSW-based Tooheys brand, was a huge client for Sutherland Smith, which also worked for the

Neil Francis (left) and Bill Harper (centre) manning the MarketMind display at a NSW market research conference.

Bond brands based in Queensland and Western Australia. The Advance Bank was one of the newly created institutions arising from the financial sector's deregulation. It acquired the State Bank of South Australia in 1995 and, in 1997, Advance Bank merged with St George Bank. The latter had also evolved from a co-operative building society and, in 2008 it was acquired by Westpac.

There had also been a significant research project undertaken in 1986 for the NSW Energy Ministry. At the time the ministry was experiencing negative community attitudes to power stations on the Central Coast. Sutherland Smith was engaged to undertake research which revealed that the community believed that the power stations were the cause of a high incidence of respiratory and asthmatic problems among children in the area. The ministry then engaged Newcastle University to undertake detailed studies to assess if emissions from the power station were contributing to the health issues. This involved setting up nephelometers and other air quality testing equipment to document wind directions and visits to doctors by children with respiratory complaints. This study showed there was no correlation between wind directions and the power stations' emissions and the researchers concluded that many of the peaks in children's visits to doctors occurred during school holidays when they were home with parents who were heavy smokers. Rod Preston, who was working with the NSW Energy Ministry at the time recalled that when the university's research was released, criticisms of the power stations ceased.

The first Sutherland Smith office was in Chatswood on the Lower North Shore, around 10km from the Sydney CBD. It was located in a commercial complex that was part of the giant Chatswood Chase retail centre. To manage the new office, Bruce and Max hired Bill Harper who had been running the Nationwide business from Sydney. Nationwide was the company Sutherland Smith used for all its interviewing work. In time, because of the ever-growing volume of weekly interviews required to sustain the continuous tracking growth, Sutherland Smith was to gradually acquire a majority shareholding in Nationwide. Bill had started his working life as a chemical engineer but wanted a career change and completed a degree in psychology. Before his time at Nationwide, he had been a senior market research officer at Amatil, the former tobacco company that became a major soft drink and snack foods conglomerate. After his time there, Bill was then appointed market research manager at Colgate Palmolive. In 1986 he joined Nationwide and had been working closely with Sutherland Smith on many of their clients before accepting the invitation to join them.

In later years, Sutherland Smith was invited to work for Sydney-based Optus, which first gained its telecommunications carrier's licence in 1991. In Melbourne, Sutherland Smith had, since the late 1980s, been working for Telecom which, from 1993 was re-branded as Telstra and, in the late 1990s was progressively transformed from a government agency to a corporation listed on the ASX. When one of its senior executives accepted an offer to join Optus in Sydney, he asked Sutherland Smith to work with him. He was prepared to pay substantially more than what Telecom had been paying for its research. The Optus account gave Sutherland Smith another large Sydney-based client. This lessened the risk of the office becoming unviable if the Bond Brewing account was lost. Optus was an exciting new venture in a sector undergoing dramatic transformation. It made extensive use of tracking research, quickly built a strong share of the Australian telecommunications market and remained a MarketMind client for some eight years.

Liane Ringham

Around the time of winning the Optus account, Bruce and Max needed to seek a new leader for the NSW business. It was growing rapidly just as Bill Harper was contemplating a reduced role due to chronic health issues. He had told Max and Bruce he needed a less stressful role in the business. Their recruitment consultant, Malcolm Cameron, identified a rising star at Frank Small & Associates (FSA) as a potential candidate. Liane Ringham had worked in her father's small but successful advertising agency after completing a degree in psychology. She had planned a career as a clinical psychologist but became disillusioned with the profession and decided to pursue a business career. After a brief period in her father's agency she became interested in market research and joined FSA. Founded in Sydney in 1964, FSA had been a leader in the Australian market. Liane had recently been appointed a director of the business and was not seeking a new position.

It was a tragic event in Liane's life that encouraged her to consider the Sutherland Smith overture. Her fiancé, James Hurst, had recently been diagnosed with terminal cancer. He was from Melbourne and wanted to spend his last days there. She had moved to Melbourne with him and the job offer entailed an induction period as acting general manager in the Sutherland Smith Melbourne office. She and James were married in Melbourne in October and he died in December 1991. In early 1992, Liane commenced her new role and it was during her time working in Melbourne that she first learned about continuous tracking, a service she had not encountered at FSA.

Liane was then appointed managing director of Sutherland Smith NSW. After her bereavement, she was pleased to return to Sydney, her home city. She recalls being underwhelmed by the Chatswood office and one of her first decisions was to move to more prestigious and better located premises in Walker Street, North Sydney. She had learned from Frank Small, a giant in the market research industry, that a business should always have 'the look of a leader' so a good office at a good address was important. Meanwhile, Bill Harper had readily accepted Liane's appointment and was happy to reduce his workload and responsibilities. He stayed with the business in its various iterations and eventually retired in late 2001.

To assist with the planned growth of continuous tracking in Sydney, Mark Hutchinson who in 1992 had joined Sutherland Smith in Melbourne as a data processing officer, was assigned to the Sydney office for three months in 1993. His work was impressive and, on his return to Melbourne, was appointed data processing manager. The growth momentum gathered pace and the Sydney office proved to be a sound investment over the coming years.

Optus was one of several new clients that were attracted to MarketMind. Other large, well-known organisations that signed up for tracking and related services included Qantas, Sydney Water, Lotteries NSW, the Australian Tourist Commission, and Frito Lay the giant international snack food business. Several were to remain as clients for many years.

The Australian Tourist Commission was aggressively promoting the nation as a tourist destination and required tracking of its advertising in its major markets, England, the United States, Japan, Taiwan and New Zealand. Since the mid-1980s when the commission's campaign featuring emerging super-star Paul Hogan gained international fame, it had pursued the rapidly growing global tourist trade.

Frito Lay was part of PepsiCo. and it had acquired the Smith's snack food brand. To promote its brands, Frito Lay introduced *Tarzos*, small toy discs that were inserted in snack food packages and were collected by children. To gauge the effectiveness of the *Tarzos* promotions, MarketMind tracked the toy market rather than snack foods. In later years *Tarzos* became collectors' items that were regularly traded online.

The strong growth required Liane to recruit additional staff and there were several appointments during 1994. These included Elizabeth Terrill, who had worked with major insurer, GIO and Les Johnson, a professor of marketing at Sydney University. His role was to manage training and development. Another appointment around this time was Kym Penhall a highly experienced researcher who had worked with several major consumer goods companies and two other market research firms.

One key appointment was a former FSA colleague of Liane's, Lawrence Ang. He had joined FSA shortly after completing his university degree. After three years at FSA he then went back to academia to undertake post-graduate and then PhD studies in advertising. He returned to the industry shortly after completing his PhD in 1995 and was appointed senior consultant and tracking manager for NSW. He tells the story of how he came to join Sutherland Smith (NSW) in Chapter 16.

Lawrence recalled working on an unusual and innovative assignment for global giant Fuji-Xerox. The company manufactured and marketed not only standard photocopiers but also a range of digital printers that were used by professional businesses such as the Snap instant printing chain. Some of these top-end printers were sold at that time for around $100,000 and they revolutionised the printing industry. Lawrence and Bill Harper were asked by Fuji-Xerox to undertake continuous tracking of the entire marketing strategy aimed at the instant printing companies. The tracking was business-to-business, not business-to-consumer which was the common form. Not only did the client want to know if the marketing was appealing to the instant printing companies, it also wanted to appeal to small business owners and others who wanted to get business cards, sales brochures, catalogues and other literature printed quickly and economically. Therefore, the printing companies and their potential clients were tracked, and Fuji-Xerox was able to run a very effective marketing campaign. In future years the shop-front printing business all but disappeared to be replaced with online services. These services also required instant printing equipment and Fuji-Xerox has remained the leader in its field.

NZ Insurance was another tracking client that Lawrence worked on with Bill Harper. The tracking showed that the insurance company's advertising was ineffectual, so the challenge was to diplomatically deliver the bad news to the client. It was not the only time when diplomacy skills were needed. Bill recalled having to advise Bond Brewing that its NSW brand, Tooheys, was being outperformed by the Victoria Bitter (VB) brand which did not even advertise in the NSW market!

The growth of the NSW business led Max and Bruce to acknowledge Liane's success by offering her equity. Then, in 1996 the name was changed to Sutherland Smith Ringham, in recognition of her pivotal role in building a strong, sustainable operation.

8

How Effective is Your Advertising?

One of the early successes of continuous tracking research was for Gillette. A global giant founded in 1901, Gillette became synonymous with men's shaving gear. It later diversified into other products including toiletries and stationery. From the early days of Sutherland Smith the company had been a major client. Max had first met senior Gillette management through his enigmatic business associate, Martin Van Herk. After Van Herk's departure, a long and productive relationship with Sutherland Smith and MarketMind followed. However, there was initial scepticism about this new, small sample continuous research until the hard evidence began to emerge.

The early research had revealed that the company's Australian market share had grown. Gillette executives queried the research because the results from other research indicated there was no change in market share. However, as Max pointed out, the other research results were at least two months old. Over that time continuous tracking showed that Gillette had taken share away from its competitors. A television advertising campaign headlined, '*The best a man can get*', was credited with driving up sales of Gillette shaving gear. The next point-in-time research showed what Max had reported was accurate and he then recommended an increase in the advertising campaign. The faith in continuous tracking demonstrated by this major international brand gave the Sutherland Smith methodology huge impetus and credibility.

In later years, Gillette launched a new shaving product named *Sensor* and it dropped the highly successful *'The best a man can get'* campaign. There was no transition from the old to the new and sales and market share slumped. Data collection by Sutherland Smith attributed the downturn to the lack of transition and Gillette accepted the need for a gradual, rather than sudden change. As Max recounted many years later: 'You can't spend five years pushing visual images at people's brains and owning that headspace and then switch to something completely different. You need a bridge from one to the other and if you don't then it's like competing with yourself.'

Another example was when HJ Heinz used English actor Robert Morley and other high-profile actors to promote their soups. Rosella, one of Heinz's major competitors, retained as its presenter Barry Humphries in his iconic Dame Edna Everage guise. It proved to be a counter-productive strategy, every time the Rosella soup commercial went to air, sales of Heinz soups increased. Because consumers saw a high-profile presenter, psychologically they associated the advertisement with Heinz.

Researching the effectiveness of beer brands' advertising was undertaken in the days when most of the Australian beer market was owned by companies controlled by two of the high-flying entrepreneurs of the 1980s, John Elliott and Alan Bond. Bond, from the early 1980s, had progressively acquired Swan in his home state of Western Australia, Tooheys in NSW and the Queensland brand XXXX (commonly called Four-X). Sutherland Smith was retained by Bond Brewing and an important benefit of its MarketMind continuous tracking was that it not only tracked the client's brand, it also tracked the competitors in the beer market. From this, clients could learn from their own and competitors' advertising and marketing. In the beer market for example, the research was able to assess the effectiveness of the opposition brands many of which were owned by Elders IXL, the company run by Elliott. Through its subsidiary, Carlton & United Breweries (CUB), it marketed many renowned brands including Foster's Lager, Victoria Bitter and Carlton.

The Foster's Lager brand had a series of television advertisements with famous sportsmen such as golfer Greg Norman and cricketer Dennis Lillee. The advertisements all had a similar theme — the Foster's drinker, a male, was at a bar and the sportsman would appear at the bar, order a drink and speak to the drinker. The Foster's drinker would fail to recognise the sportsman but would make loud-mouth comments about sport. The result? The campaign was having a negative effect. Sales of Foster's would decline whenever the advertisements went to air. Who would want to be identified with a drinker who couldn't recognise the nation's most revered sportsmen? The irony was that Elders IXL was acquiring brewing businesses internationally and Elliott was telling journalists, investors and other people that the company planned to 'Fosterise the world'.

As Max wrote in his book:

> Interestingly, some ads, in an attempt at humor, sometimes make the mistake of… depicting the target identification character as something of a 'goat'. Yet the advertiser still hopes that we will react positively to the character and what he or she is saying. These often fail and can sometimes be seen to have marked negative effects. An example of this is an ad showing a Foster's beer-drinker who is so naive he fails to recognise the famous people he talks to in a bar. As the audience, if we squirm in embarrassment at a character's naivety it makes it nigh on impossible for us to 'feel like' or want to 'be like' this character representing the brand user.[4]

Alan Bond's spectacular crash in 1991 and subsequent conviction and prison sentence for fraud are legendary and much has been published about his and others' collapses. The breweries owned by Bond Corporation were acquired in

1992 by the New Zealand based brewing giant Lion Nathan. Sutherland Smith continued, for several years, to do market research on the former Bond brands, and their competitors, for the new owner.

The research findings that highlighted ineffectual advertising often brought Max and Bruce into conflict with the people at the advertising agencies who had created the under-performing commercials. The creative teams at the agencies were all too often arrogant and inclined towards self-aggrandisement rather than serving the needs of their clients. The media buyers who purchased time and space on behalf of their clients were too often motivated by what made the greatest profits for their agencies. Apart from the creative product, the media plan was the next most significant component of the campaign mix. Sutherland Smith's continuous tracking questionnaire was specifically designed to measure advertising effectiveness on both levels. The vital measures of an advertisement's performance were the ability to be noticed (or cut-through the clutter of all advertising at the time), to accurately convey the brand name (brand awareness and recognition) and to convey the desired message about the brand, or service. In addition, there was the delivery mechanism, whether it be television, cinema, radio, newspaper, magazine, billboard or whatever medium or mix of media chosen in the campaign. During that era the premier medium was television, and the extent to which an advertiser could effectively communicate a message and compete with opposition was determined by the effectiveness of the advertisement and the media plan. In television, the most popular length of an advertisement tended to be 30 seconds. Over time, continuous tracking was to identify the crucial role that shorter length commercials (10 and 15 seconds) could play, as well as the position of the commercial in the ad break which in the 1990s typically comprised three or four 30-second advertisements. Continuous tracking was able to measure the performance of a campaign far better than any previous methodology and led to the introduction of 'topping-and-tailing' in ad breaks by securing first position during the break with a longer-length ad, and last position with a shorter ad performing the role of reminder and last impression left.

The media plan was typically expressed in terms of TARPS or 'target audience rating points' where media buyers would aim to maximise the exposure of the client's ad to the desired target audience by selecting programs and media which were most watched and consumed by that specific audience. Television was the most powerful advertising medium – and the most profitable to advertising agencies – so the weights (TARPS) included in a typical media plan were heavily weighted to television with the maximum number of TARPS the budget could afford. What continuous tracking was able to contribute to advertising evaluation was not confined to the effectiveness of an advertisement. It also shone a bright new light on the performance of the media. It showed that even if a client advertised heavily over a period of time – and a typical burst of television advertising in the 1990s would be three weeks – if a major competitor or multiple competitors advertised at the same time, the performance of the campaign would be affected by the advertising competition or clutter thus created. Furthermore – and here Sutherland Smith was indebted to the expertise of an independent media consultant Patricia (Pat) Williams, owner of Williams Media Service – in many instances the actual delivery of TARPS fell below what was supposedly scheduled, thereby further reducing the ability of the advertiser to 'cut through the clutter'. Sutherland Smith and Williams Media were to form a special, informal partnership whereby client presentations of continuous tracking evaluations of advertising campaigns were attended by Pat who would provide a detailed evaluation of the media through her product known as 'media auditing'.

It was in the early days of working for Telecom that Bruce and Max had met Pat who had worked for some of the large Melbourne advertising agencies before starting her own business in 1980. Her company had developed the unique service which she called media auditing. Bruce and Max subsequently worked with her for many years to develop new methodologies for determining the effectiveness of media buying. 'For me, the holy grail was accountability and finding out what worked and what didn't work,' said Pat. 'If you were working for a retailer or a direct response client then you could get some immediate feedback on the advertising effectiveness. But when you were working for large organisations like Telecom which had far more complex purchasing cycles, it was much harder to determine what was working. I saw the continuous tracking methodology as a means of resolving these issues.'

This was another area that brought Sutherland Smith into ongoing conflict with advertising agencies. The tracking studies for the brewery, Telecom and other clients showed that advertising and media buying agencies were making poor choices when purchasing media on behalf of clients. Much of their spending was wasted as their decisions on television advertising were made largely on TARPs rather than the clients' specific target markets. Sutherland Smith adopted the concept of 'share of voice and share of mind' which measured share of 'cut-through' relative to share of spend, making for more discerning choices in all media spending. The combination of significantly greater focus on both the performance of advertisements and media campaigns contributed to further alienation from advertising agencies, whose services had never come under such close and effective scrutiny.

One client who was cynical of advertising agencies and believed they had inherent conflicts of interest was Ian Jackson of Gillette. He recalled: 'I don't know of many other areas where so much money was thrown around with so little accountability. In those days they were getting 17.5 per cent of every dollar spent on advertising, so their aim was to maximise their clients' expenditure. Agencies were also obsessed with the concept of creativity. I think it was often creativity for creativity's sake. They would tell you how important creativity was, but I was never convinced that it was the "be all and end all" in selling products. It seemed to me that the last thing the advertising agencies wanted was an independent and objective measurement of the value of their work.' He was therefore a strong supporter of continuous tracking and its clinical ability to evaluate the true effectiveness of advertising. One revelation was the effectiveness of 15-second commercials compared with the traditional 30-second genre. The significant cost benefits pleased Gillette but not its agency!

Golden Casket, the Queensland government's lottery, appointed Sutherland Smith in 1991. Established in 1917 by a charity called the Queensland Patriotic Fund to raise funds for First World War veterans, Golden Casket was acquired by the state government in 1938. Sutherland Smith tracked the effectiveness of the Golden Casket's advertising campaigns. The research evaluated not just the content of the advertisements but also the timing – were they more effective early in the week or later? It was a few years before online gambling became a pervasive industry and state-based agencies such as Golden Casket tended to dominate the lotteries and scratch card markets.

Being awarded contracts for two large tracking studies for the ANZ bank in 1994 was another major win. One study, called *Home Track,* surveyed the bank's private customers while the other, *Biz Track,* gauged the attitudes of business customers. These proved to be flagship tracking studies for Sutherland Smith. To manage the work, a new team was formed. Jill Owen, who was previously with the National Australia Bank was recruited as senior research executive and Dianne Gardiner who had joined Sutherland Smith as a casually employed coder in 1992, was promoted to the full-time staff and was appointed group co-ordinator. Dianne's introduction to Sutherland Smith was via an agency where she was doing some casual work after completing her commerce degree. She had identified market research as her vocation.

To take on the ANZ work, Max and Bruce had to relinquish Advance Bank as a client. They had worked for the new bank from the late 1980s but in coming years it was to eventually disappear into the Westpac giant. ANZ was to remain a major client for several years.

9

A Growing Team

In mid-1990 Bruce and Max and their team left the Richmond offices and moved to Dandenong Road, Carnegie, some 12km south-east of the CBD. After several successful years the business had grown substantially, and the partners were planning to purchase their own office building. The new, two-storey, nondescript building was part of a commercial complex that

The Carnegie offices where Sutherland Smith was based from 1990.

comprised 10 individual offices on separate titles. While Max and Bruce liked the inner-city environment of Richmond and were reluctant to leave the area, the relocation was to be another important milestone in the Sutherland Smith story.

The nearby Rosstown Hotel in Carnegie – major issues were resolved there from 1990.

Soon after the move to Carnegie, the partners did manage to find a nearby hotel where

— 63 —

disputes and difficult issues could be discussed and resolved. This was the Rosstown Hotel – not a heritage listed establishment as was the Prince Alfred, their previous place of resolution, nor was there a decision table, but it adequately fulfilled its purpose. As in Richmond, all decisions were made with the support of both partners.[5]

At the time of the move from Richmond, there were around a dozen employees. As the business expanded, the numbers at Carnegie grew and, at its peak, the business employed more than 30 people in Melbourne. In addition to the researchers, this comprised data entry and data processing staff and a coding department. The new appointments included Dale Chant who is central to the story of the data processing revolution that is detailed in Chapter 12. Dale's role as a programmer was to prove a pivotal one.

Another of the key people who joined about a year after the move to Carnegie was Mark Solonsch. He had in 1989 completed an honours degree in psychology at the Australian National University (ANU) in Canberra and then worked as a market research officer at the Victorian Totalisator Agency Board (TAB). Mark had a long-time interest in gambling; he had been going to the races since he was a boy, and at 15 became Australia's youngest bookmaker's clerk. He had studied gambling behaviour at university, and around the time he joined Sutherland Smith his authoritative book on gambling was published.[6]

Research work at the TAB, which was then a state government agency, was limited so Mark sought a more fulfilling career. Through Malcolm Cameron, the recruitment agent or 'head-hunter', Mark found a position at Sutherland Smith in September 1991. Malcolm had been retained on this occasion because Sutherland Smith had recently won the Golden Casket account and was seeking a researcher with expertise in the gambling sector. Mark's knowledge and experience of the gambling markets made him attractive to Bruce and Max. It was the days before online gambling and state-owned agencies dominated the markets. Golden Casket, although Queensland-based, had hired Sutherland

A GROWING TEAM

Smith to track the effectiveness of its advertising. In the coming years, Mark's gambling knowledge helped win work from Federal Hotels which owned two casinos in Tasmania, including the nation's first at Wrest Point in Hobart. There was also work for NSW Lotteries, the TAB, Sydney Casinos and Casino Canberra. For ongoing research, none proved to be as large or as long-lasting as Golden Casket.

Originally hired to undertake qualitative work, Mark was soon engaged in both qualitative and quantitative, working with MarketMind on a range of clients, not just those in the gambling sector. He worked on the Telecom account, McCain Foods, Coles and the ANZ bank.

Romano DelBeato who joined Sutherland Smith in 1993 had been a client for some two years. He was working with Coles supermarkets and had retained Sutherland Smith to undertake continuous tracking work. After a career as a research scientist with the Bureau of Meteorology, Romano had moved into market research and was quick to appreciate the value of continuous tracking. At the time Coles was part of the Coles Myer retailing conglomerate that comprised some of the nation's best-known store brands. At the supermarkets there were mountains of data collected through cash registers and other means. Making sense of the data was an overwhelming task which he described as '... akin to attempting to drink from a gushing fire hydrant.' To get maximum value from the data, Romano hired Sutherland Smith to apply continuous tracking disciplines. He recalled: 'Like good science, the answers it provided raised many new questions and I was fully stretched exploring and explaining the results and deriving critical measures from the data such as market share.' Coles management was impressed with the outcomes and, as a result, several other businesses in the group including Kmart, Target, Officeworks and Myer committed to continuous tracking. Later, when Coles Myer invested in the World 4 Kids start-up, it used the service to monitor the national toy market. By then Romano was working at Sutherland Smith and he and Elick Teitelbaum managed the work.

In the late 1980s and 1990s, Sutherland Smith retained the services of two headhunters. Malcolm Cameron was a generalist who had, over several years, undertaken several recruitment projects for the company. He was nick-named 'the voice of doom' because of his deep voice. Dale Burrows, who had a background in the emerging information technologies sector, specialised in IT recruitment and he was instrumental in recruiting key people for MarketMind.

While continuous tracking was the growth area for the company, there was ample qualitative work being generated around the same time. Monica Greenwood was another researcher recruited to undertake qualitative work. Monica's career in market research commenced via her mother, who in the 1980s had worked at Frank Small & Associates. Monica did some part-time work at FSA while studying to become an accountant. On completing her degree, she worked at the large accounting firm, Price Waterhouse (later PricewaterhouseCoopers or PwC). Dissatisfied with the work after two years, she decided to return to FSA and do part-time interviewing and coding while she considered her future. An opportunity to do additional part-time coding at Sutherland Smith came via word-of-mouth in the early 1990s. Not long after commencing, Monica was approached by Omnia Holland who, in 1993, offered her a permanent role. The qualitative work included group taste testing of potato chips and other products for McCain Foods. Other clients included the National Gallery of Victoria and Golden Casket. While Golden Casket was largely a continuous tracking client, some of the results led to qualitative work.

Then there was the unique tracking study undertaken by Mindy Simpson, a Sutherland Smith researcher and international hockey player who competed at the inaugural indoor hockey World Cup in Germany in 2003. In 1995, whilst she was living in Europe, she sent her colleagues a regular report which she called the 'pash track'. It tracked the number of men she had kissed. Monica recalls receiving the reports that were flat in the first and second weeks and suddenly spiked in the third week, subsequently went flat and then spiked again later in the year. The laughter reverberated through the office and every new report was eagerly awaited. Peggy Duell recalled that other young staff members were inspired to start their own versions of the 'pash track', and it endured for some years. Mindy subsequently moved to Perth and practises as an endorsed organisational psychologist. She now specialises in performance enhancement in businesses, in other organisations and on the sporting field.

Both Max and Bruce attribute much of their success to the quality and commitment of the people they employed and the work environment that was created. From the time they moved to Carnegie, the partners began implementing programs designed to create a cohesive team. Every Monday at 8.30 am, the week commenced with a 'work in progress' meeting. These meetings soon evolved into staff learning sessions at which team members would be invited to make presentations on work they were doing. From the presentations there would be exchanges of views, group learning and a breaking down of the barriers that were commonplace in many professional services businesses.

A weekly staff newsletter was then introduced. As Bruce recalls; 'Max had the idea of the newsletter which he then delegated me to write. It was called *The Gazette* and it was published around 5 pm every Friday afternoon.' The newsletter served two purposes; it contained a great deal of information about the work staff were undertaking, and details of the business and its direction. The distribution of the newsletter was followed by evening drinks and social interaction.

A staff retention program was also devised. Those who wanted to enhance their skills and knowledge were encouraged to undertake short courses. All were invited to attend the annual Australian market research conference. Those who expressed an interest were asked to submit a short essay on why they would like to go and how their attendance would benefit the company. The essays were judged, and Sutherland Smith would sponsor the winner's trip to the conference.

Presentation skills training was also offered to staff. Sutherland Smith hired the services of former Channel 7 presenter and journalist, Malcolm Gray. He ran presentation skills and public speaking courses, and these were popular as staff were often required to present research findings to clients. A 'dry run' was introduced which entailed staff presenting to Bruce and Max before appearing before their clients.

In early 1992 Max was offered an adjunct professorship in marketing at Monash University. He readily accepted – his enduring connection with academia was again fulfilled, and he held the position until 2000. The role, which was not onerous, involved research, guest lecturing and supervision of PhD students. When the appointment was made, Bruce wrote in a letter to clients and colleagues; 'If looking like a Cheshire cat for the last week conveys how he feels about this, you've got the correct message that he's tickled pink.'

When Sutherland Smith moved from Richmond to Carnegie, the nation was in the grip of a deep recession. The excesses of the 1980s when rogue entrepreneurs flew high and then crashed and burned and a series of local and international economic factors created the pre-cursor for what then-Treasurer Paul Keating called, '...a recession that Australia had to have'.[7]

The recession, which generated all-time record-high interest rates and the nation's highest post-war unemployment levels, had little impact on Sutherland Smith and it emerged as a resilient, expanding and debt-free business. For Bruce, from a personal perspective, the contrast with the 1982-83 recession was dramatic. From financial distress in 1982-83 to growth, leadership and financial security less than a decade later, it had been a remarkable transformation.

10

Going Global

Having global brands such as Gillette, McCain Foods, Unilever and Beecham as clients was a major incentive for Bruce and Max to think more about extending their business internationally. They perceived immediate potential through the acceptance of the service in Australia by these international companies. The next step was to take it around the world.

Max and Bruce had earlier decided a stand-alone brand was needed to distinguish the service from the generic name 'continuous tracking' and from competition known by business names, such as Millward-Brown. The MarketMind name was thought up during a brainstorming session. Bruce and Max considered many others but MarketMind was the standout and was one they felt could be exported. The word 'Technologies' was added to emphasise the software development aspect and the innovative competitive advantage that it delivered. In April 1988 MarketMind Technologies Pty Ltd became the registered business name. In the coming years, MarketMind was to become a major player in continuous tracking in many countries. From the outset, it was seen by other research firms, and their clients, as a leader in its field and many expressed their interest in using the service. This presented several challenges, including the selection of potential licensees and the definition of 'territory' or, the area within which a licence would apply. Would it be by state – as had evolved in

Australia, but which was already creating some difficulties for existing licensees – by country, by region or by other boundaries? Paramount in their consideration was the perceived need that MarketMind retain as much exclusivity as possible and that Sutherland Smith gain the greatest return from the service, but to do so without compromising licensees' ability to maximise their use of what MarketMind had to offer.

This presented some unusual situations. For example, Frank Small & Associates had expanded its services throughout Asia, and top of the agenda was to obtain a MarketMind licence for an entire region such as South-East Asia. But for Sutherland Smith to maximise returns, it made more sense to grant a licence on an individual country basis. In the case of the USA, granting one licence for the entire country in many ways seemed to limit the potential for the service in such a large market. The same applied in Europe where the biggest and most interested potential licensees operated on a pan-European basis, rather than on an individual country basis. Ultimately the decision was taken to grant a licence that applied to a territory defined by country, meaning the whole of the USA, independent countries in Europe, Asia, South America and elsewhere.

At the same time another key issue for Max and Bruce was the considerable investment they had made in the intellectual property of their unique, continuous tracking service. The software and methodologies had been developed over several years, largely by people employed by Sutherland Smith. How could they best protect their investment? They sought legal advice from lawyers at top-tier Melbourne law firm Corrs Pavey Whiting & Byrne. Bruce and Max had an ongoing relationship with the firm having undertaken investor relations research during the 1980s for partner and company director, John Dahlsen.

As Bruce recalls; 'At first, we attempted to patent the service but we were unable to convince the authorities that ours had the required unique features to justify the granting of a patent. We believed at the time that a patent offered the greatest protection. This was how MarketMind came to be registered as an international trademark – rather than a product protected by a patent.' When the decision to grant the licence on a country by country basis was made, it became necessary to register the trademark in every country. At an estimated cost of around $500 per country, this added up to a substantial sum. They had to face the fact they did not have resources to register in 149 countries so there was no alternative but to roll out the registrations giving priority to the major countries first. In doing so they were forced to risk being pre-empted to registration of the brand in various countries. They were lucky, and as it turned out the only country in which it became a problem was France where it had been registered for a market research product that had nothing to do with continuous tracking.

Another protective measure taken was the introduction in 1990 of confidentiality agreements to be signed by all Sutherland Smith staff who worked on continuous tracking activities. The agreement was also done on legal advice.

The idea of licensing the brand had evolved from discussions with their lawyers. While Max and Bruce saw the potential for international growth, they were looking for ways to do so with low levels of risk and minimal investment – franchising or licensing appeared to offer this. For a small Australian company, setting up offices in overseas markets would have required significant capital and posed an unacceptable risk to the two owners. Originally the plan was to franchise the business in separate markets, but this too proved difficult to achieve. Franchising was a complex and costly process which was best left to fast food and other high-profile consumer brands. Licensing could be undertaken with the relatively minor costs of identifying potential licensees, making the legal arrangements and providing the licensees with training and technical support. When international opportunities presented themselves the licensing arrangement proved to be a wise and pragmatic choice.

The concept had first been adopted by Sutherland Smith in 1988 when Max and Bruce had negotiated a licence agreement with Rob Donovan, the founder of Donovan Research in Western Australia. A year after MarketMind was registered, Rob Donovan joined the board of directors. Then in 1990, Professor John

Rossiter became a director. He had first met Max in the United States in 1979 and was, by 1990, working at the Australian Graduate School of Management at the University of NSW. Both had relatively short tenures, departing in 1992 due largely to other work and academic interests.

From his days as an academic, Max liked the idea of taking sabbaticals. Academics take sabbatical leave on a regular basis to travel, study and write. His time at Kent State University in 1979-80 gave him a taste for it and he floated the idea with Bruce for him to take a sabbatical from Sutherland Smith. He told Bruce he believed he could blend a traditional sabbatical with initiatives to promote their tracking services in new, overseas markets. 'I told him I wanted to go to the United States, teach and look for business opportunities there and he supported me.'

Bruce recalled Max's request for the sabbatical:

> It was a pivotal moment in our relationship and in MarketMind's future. It's arguable whether we would have pulled it off without that key moment. My recollection is pretty much as Max has speculated. From my perspective I just sensed it was a key moment, that it was something he clearly needed to do and if he didn't the dynamic that we were creating could be either lost or compromised. Having had previous experience at running my own show, the prospect did not intimidate me although it was something I probably would have preferred not to have had to do at the time.

Max took his first, and only, six-month sabbatical from Sutherland Smith in 1989 and went to Silicon Valley, teaching at the Santa Clara University in Cupertino, California where he lectured in market research and consumer behaviour. He had met Dr Michael Munson, a Santa Clara academic at a marketing conference and Munson had invited him to apply for a visiting lecturer's role at the university.

Cupertino, in northern California's Santa Clara Valley, is a town which in the early 1970s had a population of less than 20,000. Located in the area which became known as Silicon Valley, it is where in 1976 Apple Computer (now Apple Inc) was first established by its two founders, Steve Jobs and Steve Wozniak. By the time that Max arrived, the population had grown to about 40,000 and it was one of the wealthiest cities in the United States – a result of the information technology boom. Cupertino remains the headquarters of the global phenomenon, Apple Inc. Spending time in Silicon Valley also fed Max's interest in information technology. He saw and appreciated the immense impact it was having, and would have, on all aspects of business and life in general. 'Nowhere was innovation more evident than here where you could almost hear the technological heartbeat of America.'

With all the game-changing technology occurring in Silicon Valley, Max was aware it had yet to make its full impact on the area of market research. Ironically, in the area of continuous tracking, Australia was far more advanced than the United States. He, with associates from the University of Technology in Sydney, had presented a paper on continuous tracking to the 1989 USA Marketing Science Conference and was therefore in a good position to judge. In later years he concluded that the Silicon Valley revolution was focused on the huge, multi-billion-dollar global markets and not niche applications such as continuous tracking. Many major American companies were still using annual or, at best, quarterly research to measure advertising responses, brand awareness and consumer attitudes. He looked for ways to bring MarketMind to the world's largest national economy. Max's motivation and enthusiasm was further stimulated by the support of the head of the Marketing School at Santa Clara University. Professor Shelby McIntyre was enthused by the concept of continuous tracking and he asked Max to do a presentation on his ideas to the school faculty. A life-long friendship between Max and Shelby followed.

While he was in California Max established a first, tentative foothold for Sutherland Smith continuous tracking in America. He met Martin Buncher, a researcher based in the San Diego area of Southern California. Buncher became the first North American representative but the San Diego location, which was remote from major markets, did not lend itself to the success of the service, so the agreement lapsed. Success in the United States would come, but not for another five or six years. Max also took the opportunity to travel to Boston, the world headquarters of Gillette to make personal contact with Gillette's international market research manager, Ken White. It developed into a strong relationship and Max would return to Boston every two years to maintain contact with White and other Gillette executives.

An important benefit of the sabbatical was that Max had early introduction to technologies that had yet to fully emerge. One was PowerPoint. First created in 1987 by a Silicon Valley start-up called *Forethought*, PowerPoint was originally designed for the Apple Macintosh computer. Soon after it first appeared, PowerPoint was acquired by Microsoft. It began to proliferate around 1990 and eventually became a roaring international success. Max grasped the technology very early on and was excited to be able to make slick, impressive, high-tech presentations. This was at least a year before PowerPoint started to become widely known, and as we know it became commonplace. The presentations he made on PowerPoint at that early stage bore visual testimony to MarketMind's claim to be a technology leader and helped sell the Sutherland Smith and MarketMind services. Max's love of new technologies and the timely sabbatical in Cupertino delivered this, along with a number of other competitive advantages.

And while Max was on his sabbatical, Bruce managed the burgeoning Australian operations. Both Melbourne and Sydney offices were expanding, and he was constantly travelling between the two. His challenges included new clients, new staff and a far more complex business environment. Sutherland Smith had rolled out the MarketMind entity in the previous year and was also still providing qualitative research to a wide range of clients. It was an intensive six months for Bruce.

Not long after Max returned from his Californian sabbatical, an invitation catapulted Sutherland Smith/MarketMind into the international Asian market.

Max's presentation to Frank Small & Associates took MarketMind into Asian markets.

The invitation came from the founder of Frank Small & Associates (FSA). The firm had offices and agencies in South-East Asia. Max had met Frank Small in the early 1970s when working at Coca-Cola and when he attended his first market research conference in Canberra. Small was one of Australia's most successful researchers and Max was a newcomer but, when they met at the conference, Small was happy to chat and share a beer with Max. Max was flattered that he was prepared to spend time with a newcomer. At subsequent conferences and other events, they had maintained an acquaintanceship.

In 1992 Sutherland Smith had recruited Liane Ringham for its Sydney office to eventually take up the reigns of managing director in NSW. The Sutherland Smith Sydney office had been operating since 1988 in competition with other research companies, one of which was FSA. Liane carried a message with her from Frank Small. The message conveyed by Liane was; 'Tell that Sutherland bastard who is pinching my best staff to ring me and talk to me about MarketMind.' When Max called and then went to see him, the discussion ended with Small inviting him to go to Hong Kong the following week and pitch to his FSA International group conference, adding, 'If you can convince them, you'll convince me.'

After seeing Max's hi-tech, newly minted PowerPoint presentation in Hong Kong, FSA offices in Thailand, Indonesia, Malaysia and the Philippines signed on to become licensees for MarketMind. It was the beginning of international growth for the continuous tracking service. FSA had several large international brands such as McDonald's as clients. When continuous tracking was adopted by

McDonald's in the Philippines, it was soon taken up by McDonald's franchises in other markets thereby adding to the impetus of MarketMind's international expansion. On the initial trip to Hong Kong, Max took Kingsley Winikoff as his technical expert. From that time, Kingsley assisted new licensees with technical training.

Another major international breakthrough came about a year after the FSA successes in South-East Asia. This time it was the United Kingdom. Bruce signed a licence agreement with Martin Hamblin, a major research firm based in London. The connection came circuitously from the time Bruce was working in London in the early 1970s. He had met John Wigzell, a researcher who was working with the large, international advertising agency, Ogilvy & Mather. John was on the governing council of the Market Research Society (MRS) in the UK and was asked by its Australian counterpart, the MRSA to give a series of talks about British advertising to some of the state branches here. He came to Australia and re-connected with Bruce and met Max. Impressed by what he saw when exposed to continuous tracking, he suggested Bruce give a presentation to the MRS annual conference in Birmingham. At that conference Bruce met Derek Martin, a co-founder of Martin Hamblin. The licence agreement soon followed, and John Wigzell worked part-time as a continuous tracking associate with Martin Hamblin after a three-month secondment to MarketMind in Melbourne.

Simon Friend – a key global driver of MarketMind

The international expansion gathered even greater momentum from 1996 when Simon Friend joined MarketMind. A former primary school teacher in England and New Zealand, Simon gave up teaching in the late 1970s and went to work for the brewing giant Lion Nathan in Wellington. There he was first exposed to market research. After four years he joined Market Research New

Zealand where he first experienced a basic form of continuous tracking. He then joined the international research firm SRG which posted him to Malaysia and then Hong Kong. He later returned to Malaysia and joined Frank Small & Associates. It was there that he met Max who had come to set up the MarketMind licence. The MarketMind concept appealed to Simon and he felt comfortable and confident working with it. It was Simon who opened the doors at FSA clients, McDonald's and Kodak in Malaysia.

Launching the MarketMind licence in the UK.

After five years, Simon and his wife Christine returned to New Zealand and it was then that he received an approach from Max and Bruce. From his New Zealand base, Simon became the global representative for MarketMind. His brief was to find new licensees, to educate and train newly signed licensees and to ensure that existing licensees were maximising the benefits of continuous tracking. It was Simon's enthusiasm, willingness to roam the world blended with his profound understanding and commitment to MarketMind that helped drive its globalisation. His work complemented the technical training provided by Kingsley.

Simon's years with FSA in Malaysia gave him friendly access to the Asian licensees until the FSA subsidiaries were acquired by Taylor Nelson Sofres (TNS), the large multinational research firm based in the UK. TNS was developing its own continuous tracking service and would, in the coming years, negotiate its divestment of MarketMind with another large multi-national, NFO Worldwide. Meanwhile Simon helped secure licensees in North and South America with training, advice and other support.

Ross Cooper Lund (RCL), a large and rapidly growing market research company based in Teaneck, New Jersey, first contacted Bruce and Max in 1994. RCL had a client base that included a number of major pharmaceutical companies and had apparently become aware of MarketMind through one of its clients. Max was in Boston visiting Gillette when contact was first made, and he agreed on the phone from Boston to meet with RCL executives who immediately flew to Boston to meet him at the airport prior to his return to Australia. Following that first encounter, Dave Ross, one of RCL's founders, came to Melbourne in April 1994 to meet with the Sutherland Smith team. RCL were keen to obtain a licence for MarketMind and, in 1996 a 12-month, renewable contract was arranged. Soon after, the MarketMind licence accounted for around 50 per cent of RCL's total revenue.

In September 1996 Max and Bruce held a conference of MarketMind licensees in Melbourne. Representatives from some 15 licensees attended to learn of the latest developments. It was late September and Bruce decided that the overseas guests should be exposed to some unique Australian culture. He obtained tickets to the AFL Grand Final and took the visitors to the MCG. There they saw the match between the North Melbourne Kangaroos and the Sydney Swans. It was the centenary Grand Final and more than 93,000 people attended the historic match that was won by the Kangaroos. In later years, some of the attendees recalled more about their afternoon at the football than the conference held at a city hotel.

From 1996, Simon Friend had made regular trips to RCL to help train its researchers in the MarketMind methodologies. The explosive growth of continuous tracking research in the United States was another huge boost for the international expansion of the Melbourne-based business that Bruce and Max had launched less than a decade earlier.

Meanwhile, Bruce had been seeking licensing opportunities in South America. In 1997, a day after completing his master's degree in Applied Social Research at Monash University, he travelled to Rio de Janeiro. There he attended a market research conference in search of a licensee. A firm called Indicator emerged as a potential MarketMind licensee for Brazil. He also sought an Argentinian firm, but he did not need to look further – Indicator also wanted the Argentinian licence, and this was soon agreed. The signing of Indicator in Brazil and Argentina was then followed with induction and initial training for the new licensees by Simon. The entry into South America via the continent's two largest national economies was another coup for MarketMind.

From South America, Bruce had flown to Toronto where a contract had recently been arranged with leading national firm Canada Market Research Ltd, and he worked with principal Graham Peters to do the initial induction and staff training with the firm. The Canadian licence never fulfilled expectations despite the high standing of the licensee.

By the late 1990s, MarketMind was operating in more than 20 countries in North and South America, Europe, Asia-Pacific and the United Kingdom. These included the United States, Canada, Mexico, Brazil, Argentina, England, France, Finland, Indonesia, Singapore, Malaysia, Thailand, Hong Kong, South Korea, the Philippines and New Zealand as well as the home base, Australia. The arrangement in Australia was slightly different – individual licences were held in three different states. There was the Western Australian licence with Donovan, in Victoria it was held by the parent company, Sutherland Smith, and in New South Wales the licensee was Sutherland Smith Ringham.

It was a remarkable period of growth. The licensing era had only started to become an international story in 1992 when Max was invited to address the Frank Small & Associates conference in Hong Kong. Within five years, the MarketMind brand was operating under licence in the world's largest markets.

11

THE COLUMN THAT BECAME A BOOK

The first of Max's columns in *AdNews* had appeared in 1981. *AdNews* was one of two journals servicing the Australian advertising industry, the other being *B&T*. Founded by David Yaffa in 1928, *AdNews* is believed to be one of the oldest marketing and advertising journals in the world. In the era before social media, the two publications were widely read in advertising and public relations agencies and marketing departments throughout Australia.

Max was working at McNair Anderson at the time he first submitted an article, and to his delight, it was accepted by the editor. At the time, Max had a high profile in the Market Research Society of Australia and was also well-known in the advertising industry and academia. After several more articles were submitted and published, Max was asked to write a fortnightly column. The original column was called *The Sutherland Survey*. Researching and writing a fortnightly column was onerous and, after a few months, he quit. Some time later, he decided to try again and *AdNews* welcomed the resurrected column.

With some breaks, the column ran for more than 20 years. *AdNews* published several of Max's articles when he was on sabbatical in the United States and he was asked to resume the column when he returned. There were some catchy headlines such as *Hookers for lookers; Would you like drugs with that?* and, *When sex didn't sell*. The exposure in a well-read industry journal provided powerful promotional stimulus for Max and the Sutherland Smith and MarketMind brands.

The columns covered, in considerable depth, some of the major marketing and research issues of their day and Max was always prepared to challenge conventional thinking and beliefs. The columns were also entertaining and very readable. They gained Max an international reputation when they were published in countries such as South Korea where the *Ad Age* magazine syndicated them.

With the urging of colleagues and friends, Max used the columns as the groundwork for a book, *Advertising and the Mind of the Consumer: What works, what doesn't and why*. It was first published by Allen & Unwin in 1993 and quickly became an authoritative text – and an outstanding promotional tool for Sutherland Smith and MarketMind. Not long after it was first published, the book went to third place on the best-seller list for Australian business books.

In his *Acknowledgements* section, Max gives some insights to the book's creation. There were several academics who influenced his thinking. These included Professor John Rossiter, Dr John Galloway, Larry Percy, professors Joe Danks and David Riccio, Shelby McIntyre and Dr Rob Donovan. Two non-academics who were instrumental in the development of Sutherland Smith and MarketMind are also mentioned; head-hunter Malcolm Cameron and public relations consultant Mike Hanlon. The Sutherland family is also acknowledged. As Max recalled: 'My now adult son, Kent, and daughters Keli and Julia still envy their friends whose households chatted during ad breaks whereas in ours, they now tell me, they felt they had to keep quiet "because dad was watching the ads". And whereas these other households recorded TV programs and fast forwarded the ads, their dad had to record and fast-forward through the programs to *watch* the ads. Thanks to all of them for their understanding and the time to make the book happen.'

Eventually there were to be three editions. The third edition, published in December 2008, was published in eight languages – English, Dutch, Polish, Korean, Chinese, Turkish, Indonesian and Romanian. It is held in 95 public libraries around Australia.

The profile developed from the columns and the book made Max a much sought-after speaker at seminars and other functions and something of a media commentator. The last column was published in *AdNews* in 2004 and he launched the *sutherlandsurvey* blog soon after. Like the magazine columns, the blog featured informative and entertaining articles which challenged conventional thinking and also had catchy headlines such as *Erectile dysfunction and The Da Vinci Code*; *False alarm theory*; *How humorous ads work*, *Messages in masquerade*, *Communications in camouflage* and *Emotion is a pain in the anterior cingulate*. The monthly blog also garnered a loyal international following and ran until 2010. Among the dedicated followers was Professor Shelby McIntyre who was head of the faculty when Max lectured at Santa Clara University in 1989. The beauty of the blog was that it was accessible throughout the world whereas the old-fashioned print journals, such as *AdNews*, had circulations largely limited to their home countries. By 2010 Max had grown tired of the blog and decided to terminate it. Many dedicated followers conveyed their disappointment to Max and in later years, with the benefit of hindsight, he wished he had maintained the blog.

The columns, the book and Max's leadership inspired the work of another market researcher and academic, Lawrence Ang. Shortly after hearing Max speak at an Australian Graduate School of Management seminar, Lawrence joined the Sutherland Smith (NSW) team in Sydney in 1995. He and Liane Ringham had previously worked together at Frank Small & Associates. He later returned to academia as an associate professor, Marketing at Macquarie University in Sydney. In his book, *Principles of Integrated Marketing Communications* published by Cambridge University Press in 2014, Lawrence acknowledged 'three wise men' who taught him – John Rossiter, Max Sutherland and Larry Percy. Professor Rossiter supervised Lawrence's PhD and had been a colleague and associate of Max's. Professor Percy is an American researcher and academic whose writing and work on planning provided Lawrence with a different perspective. Rossiter and Percy had also co-authored a highly regarded book *Advertising and Promotion Management*. Lawrence also acknowledged Liane Ringham and Bill Harper who he worked with at Sutherland Smith Ringham. In later years, Lawrence said the overall philosophy of his book was inspired by his time at Sutherland Smith Ringham.

12

The Data Processing Revolution

Looking back, it is clear that the single largest factor that made MarketMind an international success was the internal data programming revolution. When Bruce and Max first decided to pursue continuous tracking, they had retained external consultants to develop the highly specialised software required for the task. This proved frustrating and unsuccessful. They would brief consultants and typically the responses addressed only half of what had been asked. There were many other shortcomings so, in the late 1980s, the pair decided to employ data programmers in the belief that people who were exposed to the day-to-day needs of market research, and were employed to focus on a single task, would have a greater chance of success.

Dale Chant: from ancient Greek history to MarketMind's pivotal programmer

Eventually there were three key appointments – Kingsley Winikoff, Roland Seidel and Dale Chant. Kingsley had a long history in the IT sector going back to his time with IBM in the 1960s. Roland, whose background was mathematics, was also a former teacher but it was Dale who had the most unusual background and career. His story and contribution are remarkable. As he recalled:

> I answered an ad from Dale Burrows, the Sutherland Smith recruitment consultant, sometime in the late 1980s for a technical writer. I had been playing around with first-generation home computers since the early 1980s, and I wrote decent enough prose, so technical writing seemed a possibility. As it happened, the job advertised was for IBM mainframes – completely out of my league, so I withdrew, but Dale said come in for an interview anyway. He made notes, and said if anything came up, he'd let me know.
>
> In 1988 I had obtained a position at St John's Greek Orthodox College, Preston, teaching Year 12 ancient Greek history. Just before the 1989 Christmas and New Year break, our computer teacher was hijacked by an industry offer. The principal called a meeting and asked, 'Who knows anything about computers?' As the only responder, I suddenly found myself in charge of a network of early Mac machines and a Year 11 class to teach the wonders of programming. Year 11 I could handle, but after a quick review of the Year 12 syllabus I realised I needed to seriously upgrade my computing skills from marginal to at least adequate or I would be doing a disservice to the school and my students.
>
> So, it was back to university for my fifth academic qualification (BA Tasmania, BA hons Monash, PhD Monash, DipEd Melbourne, and now Diploma Computer Science, Melbourne). The Dip Computer Science course was a graduate level course – you had to have at least honours in a technical field like maths or physics to even be considered, but they made an exception

for me based on a personal interview. This was the hardest academic work I had ever done; 120 of us started the course – 30 finished. Pre-fees, the role of the academic was to weed out the weak as soon as possible, and not (as now) to keep them on as long as possible.

Towards the end of this course, in late 1990, I got a call from Dale Burrows asking if I was interested in working in market research. 'What's that?' I asked. He briefly explained, I said OK and next thing I knew I was being interviewed by Max, who offered me a position, initially to learn the ropes in data processing and then to write a custom software suite to implement the MarketMind tracking methodology. I resigned from St John's, and commenced at the Sutherland Smith office in January 1991.

The first six months were hell. I was finishing the diploma in evening classes, my wife was having a difficult pregnancy and birth of our second child, I was teaching evening classes for Melbourne TAFE to make ends meet, I was having legal issues over a previous business venture and I knew nothing about IBM PCs, having worked only on Amiga, Apple Mac and Sun work-stations. Instead of spending the evenings mastering Surveycraft and MS-DOS, I was either teaching at TAFE or debugging assignments. I think they nearly sacked me, but by mid-year things had cleared up enough for me to get properly stuck into the main task, and by year's end I had the bare basics of the MarketMind software in place. It soon became clear that the scope of the task was beyond a single inexperienced programmer, so I prevailed on Max and Bruce to appoint a friend and my computing mentor, Roland Seidel, as basically the system architect. I handled the survey interface side (crosstabs, data processing), and he handled things like memory allocation routines, stats algorithms, class structures, etcetera. Between us within twelve months we had a working and licensable system, which Max and Bruce then took to the world.

One day, well after he had joined the firm, Dale asked Max why he had been prepared to hire him. Dale realised he was an unconventional choice and was puzzled as to why Max ever thought him a worthwhile prospect. Dale recalled Max's response:

- I'm a sucker for anyone with a PhD.
- Your thesis was essentially an account of persuasion (sophistry) in ancient Greek drama, and analysing persuasion is the business of FMCG (fast moving consumer goods) advertising market research.
- You had hands-on experience with running a business. (This was a small independent record label and music retailing business from 1985-88. It was not a successful enterprise, ending in tears and me being sued – but to Max some blood on the floor was a pro, not a con).
- You had hands-on experience with advertising. (Actually, this was mostly being apprehended by the police while putting up posters around town at 3 am, but again, Max saw that as a pro).
- You transitioned from hard-core arts/humanities to hard-core hi-tech – very few can do that, and since advertising is all about themes and language and message-making, you can make semantic links on how to implement the methodology as software that others won't see.
- You had done a year (1984) at the Victorian Government Ministry of Consumer Affairs, so had experience with the consumer point of view.
- You were highly motivated, literate and flexible, thereby ticking the traditional personnel boxes too.

The overall task was to write a software suit to implement the MarketMind tracking methodology. The original processing chain was Surveycraft->Lotus123->Harvard Graphics. In the early days, it took weeks to get the client reporting out the door, by which time the results in the FMCG (fast moving consumer goods) markets were already ancient history. The envisaged MarketMind software would do all three steps as a single, seamless and transparent process. The first released version was MS-DOS. This was rebuilt for Windows 3.2 16 bit, and then for Win 95 32 bit.

To meet the aims of seamless and transparent, the software had to subsume many data processing tasks, so it grew in scope until all standard processing, except data collection, was accommodated. The programmer would feed Surveycraft, or other raw case data files in, and a deck of presentation-ready charts would come out. If something did not look right the analyst could check each sub-process along the way. In tracking, things could always go wrong. We went from weeks for client reporting to close-of-wave on Friday and reports in the mail by Monday afternoon.

Dale recalls the tutelage he received from Kingsley Winikoff. 'He had a genius for spotting a glitch or diagnosing a problem and a deep instinct for how computers can misbehave. He was as smart as they come, played the violin, was never unreasonable and a great line manager.'

There were other memories that he treasured. 'There was none of the vast waste in effort I saw when at much bigger enterprises like the Victorian public service and later NFO Worldwide and TNS. Everyone was focussed and productive. No dills allowed!'

The freedom to come and go as he pleased was another positive memory that several of his colleagues also mentioned in their recollections – office hours were flexible. Dale said the art of programming required 'large slabs of pure thinking and uninterrupted time', and this was better obtained by working from home than at the office.

The tight-knit work environment was also beneficial. 'The typical frustrations of programming such as poor briefs leading to useless apps were never in evidence. We deployed DevOps at its finest. Our users were right there, and if they didn't like something, they could explain why, and we fixed it more or less immediately. Progress was very rapid and tightly focussed. Gillette was our on-running test case. Lion Nathan had a job with 25 years back data. Getting that into the MarketMind system liberated the analysts.'

Dale recalled the 1990 recession and its aftermath. 'There was the recession in the early 1990s, but it did not have much of an impact on Sutherland Smith. But by 1995 the effects of globalisation and international competition were starting to bite. Millward-Brown were giving us some grief in the methodology wars. Computer technology and programming languages were evolving rapidly so there was a constant challenge.'

The sale of the Victorian business in 1996 was a shock and he said the reason given was that try as they might, Sutherland Smith could not get off the revenue plateau it had been on for several years while costs were constantly increasing. While some of the staff were not happy and made remarks like 'traded as so much horse flesh', they did get to work in a much larger company, and none was retrenched. This left Max and Bruce free to concentrate on the global marketing of the MarketMind methodology. Around this time the MarketMind team comprised 10 staff and was a mix of market researchers and programmers. Dale Burrows was appointed general manager – operations and his duties covered local and international administration and development of the MarketMind activities.

The sale of MarketMind to NFO in 1998 was a life-changer for Dale Chant and several others. He recalled Max calling a meeting and telling the team that included himself, Roland Seidel, Mike McCarthy, Neil Francis and Dale Burrows that there was 'a big bonus if you move to New Jersey for two years minimum.' The rationale was NFO had no confidence in a small development team in a remote part of the world and wanted a technology transfer to a USA team with in-built redundancy against personnel movements. While NFO had made the acquisition, the day-to-day management of MarketMind was in the hands of Ross Cooper Lund. 'They sent us all to stay at the Teaneck Marriott hotel next door to RCL for a month to get oriented, meet the RCL personnel and arrange housing. NFO did not have a clue about how to relocate whole families – we were left on our own to try to sort it all out. Arranging work visas alone was one nightmare among many.'

The relocation plans, largely because of costs, fell apart, so Dale presented a compromise solution to Max, Bruce and Rick Lund. As he had designed the MarketMind software, he proposed that only he and his family relocate. This reduced the costs by four fifths, delivered similar outcomes, and so was agreed.

Dale recalled the transition: 'We arrived in New Jersey in May 1999. My job was to assemble a programming team and get them familiar with the software so that if Roland or I ceased to be available, the MarketMind enterprise could nonetheless continue. Two Australians, Kate Platter and Sally Campbell, were also there for the methodology and sales side, replacing the roles originally envisaged for Neil Francis and Dale Burrows. The two new people came to NFO via the Stochastic methodology purchase. At the end of the two years, my job done, I returned to Melbourne. The MarketMind office had moved to Glen Waverley. I continued to work mostly from home, and by now email was the primary means of communication.'

According to Dale, things were going smoothly, and the MarketMind Version 5 was in final testing before release. 'Then NFO, which had been acquired by the Interpublic Group of Companies in 2000, was suddenly put up for sale and eventually purchased by TNS – the worst possible choice from our point of view because TNS had been forced by competitive circumstances to develop a rival product that they called Miriad. They naturally argued that Miriad was the better system so MarketMind had to go. There followed an epic farce as the two systems were evaluated in a bake-off, with the forgone conclusion that we were retrenched.' With that, MarketMind was buried.

Roland and Dale both had more than six months accrued leave. That, plus other termination payouts, gave them the seed money to take what they had learned about survey data analysis and tracking, and to generalise it into a commercial package they could sell to any agency in need of advanced tracking or other analytics. Because the system was capable of implementing any methodology, there were no intellectual property issues. Roland and Dale set up Red Centre Software to develop and market the Ruby survey and data analysis suite. They have been running this as an ongoing business since 2006 and Ipsos is their major client. Many ex-NFO people who were unhappy with the sale to TNS had, in the meantime, moved to Ipsos, so Roland and Dale had personal contacts and internal champions to promote their cause. As Dale sums up; 'Thus did we rise from the ashes.'

Sadly, Kingsley died in February 2009, aged 67. He had retired in early 2004 just as the Melbourne MarketMind office was closing. He had talked about finding some part-time work, but his great love of music and volunteering kept him busy and provided a good quality of life. He and his wife Judy were also able to travel during this period. Then, in October 2007 he was diagnosed with oesophageal cancer and passed away in 2009. Among the very last people to see him alive, according to his widow Judy, were two of his old colleagues, Bruce and Peggy.

13

Peggy's Boiler Room

According to Max and Bruce, the success of Sutherland Smith and MarketMind was in no small part due to the exceptional staff that came on board and the work environment that the company culture somehow nurtured. In addition to Dale Chant and the programming team, another person played a central role in the success story. This was Peggy Duell – controller of what they called 'the boiler room' – a quaint name for the internal engine that drove the businesses.

Peggy Duell.

Peggy joined Sutherland Smith in 1987. She was one of the early appointments after Max and Bruce relocated to Richmond in 1986. She had planned to stay for only a brief period but remained well after the sale of MarketMind in 1998. Peggy first met Max when he was working in Jolimont Terrace and she worked in an adjoining building. It was a passing acquaintanceship and she had no idea of his work even though she was in an allied field. She was employed by the associate company Nationwide Research Services. Her role there was interviewing on the continuous tracking questionnaires as well as in-depth interviewing and general administration.

When Sutherland Smith moved to Richmond, Nationwide also relocated there. Peggy saw Max on the stairs one day and asked, 'What are you doing here?' He replied grandly, 'I own the place.' Peggy's abilities were soon noticed, and she was invited to work part-time with Sutherland Smith as Max's personal assistant. This was in addition to her work at Nationwide. At the time, all coding and data entry was being done in Sydney. Max and Bruce decided the work, for quality control reasons, should be done in Melbourne. Max asked Peggy if she would also like to do the coding. She recalls being given a large pile of questionnaires and a packet of post-it® notes. 'Each note had four lines "ad, item, brand, message". That was my introduction, I had no idea of what I was doing. A coder came down from the Sydney office and spent a day with me. It all went from there.'

She is remembered by ex-Sutherland Smith and MarketMind people for her administrative and organisational skills as well as her directness and feistiness.

Max fondly remembers Pegg'sy unique attributes:

> Her genuine charm was a big factor in the smooth running and productivity of Sutherland Smith and MarketMind. Her ever-reliable ability to get things done increased my own productivity. Her ability to step in and manage issues that would otherwise soak up my attention was invaluable. She also had great judgement as to when an issue really demanded my attention. She was 'up-front' with people and this engendered trust. People trusted her and opened up to her, so she had an early detection radar that sensed when trouble was brewing that

might compromise the efficient functioning of the organisation. With early warning and a little applied attention, the inevitable gripes and fire spots that break out in any organisation could be more quickly dealt with and resolved. The uniqueness of this and the culture it helped nurture is something that has only became fully obvious to me in retrospect.

The method of tracking in the early days included some rudimentary technology. Peggy recalled going home after a day's work, inserting a VHS tape in her recorder and taping programs that contained advertisements being tracked. The following day she would erase the program and retain the advertisements. The technological development was rapid, but it was the team that Peggy best remembers:

> Max and Bruce were very good at recruiting quality people. They looked for people who were contributors, who understood their client's needs. This was evident in my years there. You could rely on people to be in the office at 11 o'clock at night if there was a report with a short deadline that had to be completed. We had people who would complete the word processing and then drive out to Tullamarine with the reports which would be lodged with the air freight despatch.
>
> It was an inclusive environment where people knew the value of the work that each colleague was doing. I remember watching people come into the organisation and quickly become part of a team. Some were straight out of university and you could see their development. This wasn't only due to Bruce and Max; it was also due to the key personnel who had the drive and interest in what they did to maximise the quality of the work. It was all about giving the client what they needed, not what they wanted.
>
> Over the years I recall many very young people joining such as Diane Gardiner, Monica Greenwood, Mindy Simpson

and others. You just knew they would succeed – they had the intelligence, drive and commitment – and they were nurtured.

Soon after Peggy joined, Kingsley Winikoff came on board. He was, according to Peggy, universally popular. 'He was both a gentle man, and a gentleman. He was old-fashioned, respectable, honest, highly principled and non-judgemental. Everybody found him to be a wonderful teacher who forgave mistakes.'

She also remembers Simon Friend who had joined in 1996 and came into the office from time to time and kept everybody highly entertained. 'He was the most enthusiastic person that I have ever met in my life. You could not have found a more enthusiastic person if you could have created one out of clay!' Based in New Zealand, Simon spent many months of the year travelling as the global representative for MarketMind.

And what of Peggy's memories of working with Max? 'Max was one of those totally focused people – he would not have known that the office was on fire until his keyboard started to melt!'

Another early appointment was Effie Damaskopoulos who was originally hired for the Fax 'N Figures business. When the Sutherland Smith business expanded more rapidly than predicted, Fax 'N Figures was re-absorbed into the main business because the growth demanded its full-time support. Effie became Bruce's personal assistant and worked closely with Peggy. At the time Bruce had yet to transition to computer technology for his own work. He would write laboriously in a foolscap-size notebook and Effie would then type his material on her PC. Peggy and Effie were also responsible for the retention of archival materials. They would regularly drive to a storage facility in Dandenong where they would enter a basement carpark and drag the archive boxes into a storage room at the back of the carpark. It was a large industrial site, and while the boxes were being stored or retrieved, there were large trucks constantly roaring up and down the nearby ramps.

Peggy also recalled the evening that she and Effie were working on an urgent document that had to be sent interstate. After the document had been typed and was to be photocopied, the pair were alarmed when the photocopier broke down. They meticulously pulled it apart and reassembled it and hours later were relieved when it again functioned. The project was duly completed, and Peggy and Effie left the office very late that night.

Another colleague who remembered the travails of photocopying was Mindy Simpson who joined Sutherland Smith in 1993. Administration was her first role which included the weekly photocopying of huge volumes of questionnaires for Optus. These were sent to Sydney in an overnight bag. On her first or second shift, Mindy managed to destroy many of the questionnaires and feared she would be dismissed. In subsequent weeks, while Mindy toiled, the courier was kept waiting for up to an hour and would be offered a meal to appease him. Mindy was later appointed as a research assistant and worked with the firm until 1996.

As staff numbers increased, a diary was introduced at the reception desk in Richmond. People were expected to sign in each morning, sign out when going to an appointment and sign in again on their return. Peggy recalled Max and Bruce regularly signing out together and listing their destination as 'OTR' which stood for 'over the road' – and this indicated that they were meeting at the decision table in the Prince Alfred Hotel. These meetings were rarely interrupted, even by Peggy or Effie.

While Bruce's dedication to his beloved Richmond Football Club led to extensive banter amongst staff, Peggy and several others were Geelong supporters and would often go to watch their team play at the MCG or Waverley Park. In the Sutherland Smith and MarketMind years, many marquee games were played at Waverley Park in Melbourne's east. The trips to the football became family affairs and further strengthened the bond that existed in the workplace. Many of these friendships endured long after the 1996 and 1998 sales.

After the 1996 sale of Sutherland Smith Victoria to Frank Small & Associates, Peggy worked exclusively with MarketMind. Its sale in 1998 was the beginning of a grieving process for her and others. 'With Max and Bruce and others gone, we were down to five or six people. They did their job and were good at it, but it was never the same.'

In June 2000 Peggy was appointed administrative director of the Melbourne office. The appointment was announced by Richard (Rick) Lund who had the title of Global Champion of MarketMind. He explained her role as; 'Among her responsibilities will be to maintain communication with all NFO MarketMind licensees, manage the day-to-day operation of the NFO MarketMind Melbourne office and to implement general business decisions made from Teaneck. Peggy will report to Rick Lund. We congratulate Peggy on her success to date, and on her new promotion.'[8]

The sale of NFO Worldwide to Taylor Nelson Sofres had led to the eventual abandonment of the MarketMind brand and closure of the Melbourne office. Peggy was the last person to leave. 'I turned off the lights, locked the door and walked out in 2005,' Peggy recalled. 'What had started as a six-month, part-time job went for eighteen years.'

14

Selling the Businesses

Bruce and Max had always been willing to consider offers to acquire their businesses and the occasional approach had been forthcoming but always based on offers of shares rather than cash. Based on professional advice, the pair rejected share offers, they were only prepared to consider cash offers. Around this time, an offer based on shares was made by a large, listed company that had already acquired another significant research business. Soon thereafter the company ran into difficulties – the share price nosedived and the company ultimately folded – a salutary lesson and close call for Max and Bruce.

In all there were three businesses that were eventually sold; the Sutherland Smith business in Victoria, Sutherland Smith Ringham in NSW and MarketMind Technologies Pty Ltd. All three sales were ultimately undertaken with the complete support and agreement of Bruce and Max.

The Sutherland Smith Victorian business was acquired in 1996 by an old associate – and local competitor – Frank Small & Associates. Ironically, FSA's chief executive and part-owner in Victoria was Kevin Sharp, Bruce's former partner from the early 1980s. After establishing his own business, which he then partnered with his wife, Chris, he sought growth opportunities, and this had resulted in him merging with FSA in 1986. Under this arrangement Kevin received 40 per cent equity while the business retained the Frank Small & Associates name. At the time of the Sutherland Smith acquisition, FSA had a staff of 36 in Victoria while Sutherland Smith had 27 employees.

FSA had been operating in Victoria from 1978 and had a significant presence in the Victorian market. Outside Australia, FSA was the first MarketMind licensee holding some dozen international licences in South-East Asia. While it had a strong MarketMind presence in South-East Asia it had no access to the service in Australia. That, and a perceived need for growth, were the main motivations for purchasing the Sutherland Smith business. Gaining the MarketMind licence in Victoria, plus associated qualitative work, substantially increased its revenues in the Victorian market.

A year earlier the entire FSA group had been acquired by the French-based international group, Sofres Worldwide. Sofres, the original MarketMind licensee in France, was seeking global expansion and encouraged its businesses to seek growth opportunities in their local markets. While FSA was highly profitable in the Victorian market, it was seen by Sofres as a tiny business and Kevin was urged to expand. This ultimately led to his offer and the Sutherland Smith acquisition. A year after the purchase, Sofres, merged with another giant, Taylor Nelson to become Taylor Nelson Sofres. Then, towards the end of 1998, Kevin and Chris retired.

The sale of the Sutherland Smith business in Victoria, which was announced in late 1995, came as a shock to the Victorian team. As part of the terms of the sale, Max and Bruce negotiated a guarantee that all staff could stay employed by FSA for two years. Despite this, members of the team described the weeks following the news as a time of grieving. Under its new ownership, Sutherland Smith and MarketMind were separated and operated from two, eastern suburban locations – the former in the Hawthorn office of FSA, the latter in the previous Sutherland Smith headquarters in Carnegie. Some key people chose to depart at the time or soon after the sale, including Omnia Holland, Romano DelBeato and Mark Solonsch. For Mark, who recalled several meetings with FSA managing director

Garry Young, the change 'just didn't feel right' and he left to start his own research business and then worked in several corporate research roles. Of those who chose to depart at that time, most continued in the sector and had successful careers – either with other firms or in their own businesses.

Peggy Duell recalled the staff meeting at which the sale was announced. 'It was the best-kept secret of my time there. There was total devastation – nobody had anticipated the sale. By then I had switched over to MarketMind which I knew would keep going. To me, it was another step, another direction to take. There was relief that Max and Bruce had taken care of the staff but, for the next few weeks it was very quiet and subdued.'

The New South Wales business was acquired by part-owner Liane Ringham in 1998. She had been managing director since 1992 and soon after had received equity in the business. The name had been changed in 1996 from Sutherland Smith (NSW) to Sutherland Smith Ringham. After acquiring the entire business, she decided a new beginning was required and in 2000 rebranded it Inside Story Knowledge Management. In the same year she moved the office from North Sydney to Barrack Street in the heart of Sydney's CBD where it remained for around 15 years. A brief merger with an American company followed but after less than two years a demerger was mutually agreed and in September 2017, she relocated to Martin Place, not far from the Barrack Street address. She retained – and grew – a client base of blue-chip organisations such as Sydney Water, Medibank, IAG, Westpac bank and many others.

This was a time when mergers and acquisitions were common throughout the market research and allied sectors. The Taylor Nelson purchase of FSA was just one of many. With its international success, the MarketMind business was highly likely to attract offers. A continuous tracking competitor, Millward-Brown, had shown interest in MarketMind, but an offer never materialised. Millward-Brown had itself been acquired by the global advertising, marketing, public relations and market research conglomerate WPP. Throughout the 1990s and into the new millennium, the pace of globalisation increased with large, multinational organisations making lucrative offers to smaller players. It was also a time of unprecedented change in the information technology and telecommunications industries. The era became known as the 'dot-com boom'. With the internet becoming accessible to households, businesses and the entire community, many start-up IT and telecommunications businesses were launched. Few survived into the new millennium and the boom of the 1990s did burst in the early 2000s. This era certainly had a major impact on most businesses, including market research. One 1998 start-up did more than survive. That year, two students at Stanford University, Larry Page and Sergey Brin, launched an internet business which they called *Google*.

The licence arrangement that had been struck in the United States with Ross Cooper Lund (RCL) in the mid-1990s proved to be the catalyst that led to the sale of MarketMind which was, by 1998, operating in more than 20 countries including the United States. RCL was a rapidly expanding business when it attracted the attention of another, much larger research company that was also on an aggressive growth path.

NFO Worldwide Inc. was a public listed company when, in March 1998, it simultaneously acquired Ross Cooper Lund and MarketMind. NFO had listed on the NASDAQ (the second USA stock exchange) in 1993. It subsequently listed on the New York Stock Exchange in late 1997. Founded in Toledo, Ohio, in 1946, NFO was originally known as National Family Opinion. By the time it acquired MarketMind, NFO was based in Greenwich, Connecticut and had been on the acquisition trail for most of the 1990s. It had expanded throughout North America and internationally becoming the largest market research company in the United States and one of the largest in the world. As a result of the acquisition, RCL became a division of NFO.

In its public statements, NFO explained the acquisitions as a key part of its strategy to accelerate growth in the $400 million global continuous-tracking market. It saw MarketMind as a world-class service that would help it achieve its objectives. In a press release NFO said:

Australia-based MarketMind's tracking and data-integration system delivered continuous interactive information to help marketers manage their brands more effectively. The MarketMind system was licensed in 20 countries and supported hundreds of brands. The research-based consulting firm of Ross Cooper Lund, a U.S. MarketMind licensee, conducted large-scale studies to help clients diagnose brand communications and optimise media budgets.[9]

Eight months after acquiring MarketMind, NFO announced it had awarded licences to its affiliate companies, the MBL Group in the Middle East and Asia, and BJM Research in the UK. This was a major decision as the licences were previously held by rival firm Taylor Nelson Sofres and the Frank Small & Associates Asian subsidiaries. NFO had negotiated the re-assignment of MarketMind licences with Taylor Nelson Sofres which had acquired Frank Small & Associates in 1995. In its media release, NFO announced that: 'The reassignment of the licenses was concluded by mutual agreement between NFO Worldwide and Taylor Nelson Sofres.' The agreement included the Victorian MarketMind licence that had been acquired in 1996 as part of FSA's purchase of Sutherland Smith Victoria. One month later, NFO also acquired Donovan Research in Western Australia, the very first non-Sutherland Smith firm to become a MarketMind licensee in 1988. This gave NFO two separate licences in the Australian market.

Simon Friend remained with MarketMind after the NFO acquisition. He regarded MarketMind in Asia, Asia-Pacific and South America as 'his baby', and he continued to work on the roll-out in these and other regions for more than three years. Eventually, he grew disillusioned with the NFO modus operandi and the demanding international travel schedules and he departed.

Meanwhile in Melbourne, NFO announced a new regime commencing from June 2000. The announcement was made by Rick Lund, another RCL founder who, after the acquisition of his company, had been appointed global managing director, NFO MarketMind. Peggy Duell was appointed administrative director and other former Sutherland Smith staff including Kingsley Winikoff, Dale Chant, Roland Seidel and Neil Francis had their roles re-defined.

Kingsley, who was global technical support coordinator, was to oversee and advise NFO's regional technical support managers and report directly to the new chief technology officer for NFO MarketMind. Dale and Roland were to continue in their roles as co-project managers but would also report to the new chief technology officer. Neil Francis who had several roles including marketing director, also had new reporting lines.

The imminent retirement of Bruce Smith and resignation of Dale Burrows, the former recruitment consultant who in 1997 had been appointed general manager, operations, were also covered in the announcement.

That same year, only two years after its MarketMind and RCL acquisitions, NFO itself was acquired for $US611 million by the huge, New York-based, international advertising and marketing conglomerate, the Interpublic Group of Companies Inc. (IPG). It too was listed on the New York Stock Exchange and had offices in more than 100 countries. Interpublic subsequently sold NFO to Taylor Nelson Sofres which, in turn was acquired by the global research giant Kantar. The cycle of merger and acquisition was, and remained, never-ending.

The sale of the Sutherland Smith and MarketMind businesses by 1998 signalled the end of the successful and happy partnership between Max and Bruce. It had commenced as a de facto partnership in 1984 and flourished from then until the divestments. Under the terms of the RCL and NFO buy-outs of MarketMind, they continued to work with the new owners. Max was based in California while Bruce was based in Melbourne. This was a relatively brief post-sale arrangement when they supported NFO with the identification and sale of new licences and guidance on the MarketMind processes. But it was also the time for them to separately plan their futures. While their bond remained strong, there was no further need to arrange meetings at the decision table, or the local pub – except for nostalgia reasons.

15

After Sutherland Smith

A number of successful businesses and successful people were spawned from Sutherland Smith and MarketMind. The sales of 1996 and 1998 triggered several start-up businesses by former employees. Most felt the knowledge and experience they gained at Sutherland Smith and at MarketMind had prepared them well for their own enterprises. Some launched their businesses soon after their departures, others worked elsewhere beforehand.

Liane Ringham acquired the NSW business in 1998 and rebranded it Inside Story Knowledge Management in 2000. Soon after the sale of the Victorian business to FSA, Romano DelBeato partnered FSA's departing managing director Garry Young to establish DelBeato Young. Garry died in 2005 and the business was subsequently renamed DBY Research. Omnia Holland launched OmniCom Research in 1997 and worked with Dianne Gardiner who briefly joined DelBeato Young and then went to OmniCom. In 2007 Dianne founded her own firm, Latitude Insights, which eventually merged with Bastion to become Bastion Latitude where she continues as chief executive officer. A former Sutherland Smith colleague, Monica Greenwood joined Dianne at Latitude Insights in 2009 and continues to work at Bastion Latitude. Stephen Prendergast founded Prescience Research in 2004 after working with Millward-Brown and

Wallis Market and Social Research. In 2006, Roland Seidel and Dale Chant set up Red Centre Software to develop and market the Ruby survey and data analysis suite.

Most give a great deal of credit for their successful enterprises to their time at Sutherland Smith and MarketMind.

Today, with hindsight, Max sums up the story of Sutherland Smith/MarketMind: 'We were a market research start-up with intellectual property in a new methodology, continuous tracking – and that opened up the opportunity to become a global player through global licensing. The sheer volumes of data that the methodology generated drove the company to innovate and morph into a software development company as the only way to grapple with the 'big data' problem.'

Big data is now a recognised field. It is described as: '…a field that treats ways to analyse, systematically extract information from, or otherwise deal with data sets that are too large or complex to be dealt with by traditional data-processing application software.'[10] This would be very familiar to anyone who worked for Sutherland Smith/MarketMind. Dale Chant recalled that Lion Nathan, the NSW brewer, had a job with 25 years of back data. 'Getting that into the MarketMind system liberated the analysts.'

In retrospect, Sutherland Smith/MarketMind was a forerunner – a pioneer in 'big data' in a market research context. The software development was driven by the need to handle the large databases that the methodology created, and the aim was to enable instant analysis of those databases. The focus was on market research, but the tools were generalisable to other data including the events file. The software development addressed the need to be able to make sense of large volumes of data. By 1998 the company had not only developed cutting edge tools with the ability to store and instantly interrogate continuous tracking databases, the development had also taken baby steps into automatic analysis – otherwise known and lauded today as AI (artificial intelligence).

The corporate name Sutherland Smith and the brand name MarketMind disappeared over two decades ago so what has occupied Max and Bruce since they sold their businesses? They have pursued personal interests and have also made enduring contributions to important societal issues of the 21st century such as health and education, wellbeing, social cohesion and end-of-life choices and challenges.

The Smith family has a long-standing association with Point Lonsdale on the Bellarine Peninsula, south-west of Melbourne. For many years they have owned a holiday house there. After the sale of the businesses, Bruce became deeply committed to the Point Lonsdale Surf Lifesaving Club. He held several positions including vice-president marketing, Rip View Swim Classic organiser and chair of the building committee which oversaw significant renovations to the back-beach base and the building of a new facility at the Santa Casa beach in nearby Queenscliff. Bruce has also made a significant contribution to Christ Church Grammar School in South Yarra where he served as a school councillor which oversaw significant building works, and served a term as president of the Parents & Friends Association.

The Tommy Hafey Club was launched in 2003. It describes itself as a business networking and support group for the Richmond Football Club, and was named in honour of the former player and legendary coach who led Richmond to four premierships between 1967 and 1974. He died of cancer in 2014 aged 82. It was Bruce who, with a couple of friends, set up the club. It was modelled on the Dick Reynolds Club which was established in 1996 in honour of the great Essendon player and coach. Bruce's friend Ray Sneddon, a sports promoter and dedicated Essendon supporter, was a founder of the Dick Reynolds Club and he was happy to share his knowledge and experience with Bruce.

The club runs several functions each year at some of Melbourne's most prestigious venues and profits are donated to the football club.

In December 2018, the club awarded Bruce the *Alice Wills Award* for 'outstanding volunteer service to the Tigers over many years.' Alice Wills was an inspirational volunteer with Richmond for more than 50 years and the annual award named in her honour recognises the exceptional contributions made by long-serving volunteers. Alice died in 2014 aged 93.

In 2004 Bruce was contacted by an old friend, the highly successful businessman Peter Scanlon. Bruce had first met Scanlon when both were studying commerce at Melbourne University. They played football there and both joined HJ Heinz after graduating. For 12-18 months they shared a flat in the eastern suburb of Chadstone before Bruce married Sue –and Scanlon moved to the United States to further his career.

For many years a senior executive and director of major companies, Scanlon had been involved in some high-profile business deals in the 1980s and 1990s. In 1984 when the elite football competition was being restructured, he was appointed one of the inaugural VFL/AFL commissioners.

He had established the Scanlon Foundation in 2001 which had as its mission '…to enhance and foster social cohesion in Australia.' A strong supporter of multiculturalism, he was inspired by the generations of immigrants who came to Australia, built new lives for their families and made immense contributions to the nation.

Scanlon told Bruce he wanted the foundation to do comprehensive, ongoing research on immigration to Australia. Bruce was appointed Social Cohesion Research Program Coordinator and has worked with the foundation since that first meeting. With the support of academics and leaders in multiculturalism, a detailed program of research was designed and implemented over 12 to18 months. It culminated in a decision to run a regular national survey and publish reports that gauged the attitudes of Australians to immigration. The survey would also measure what was then a relatively unknown concept, social cohesion. Now a well-known term, social cohesion measures overall community wellbeing and integration.

Working with the Social Research Centre, Monash University and the Australian Multicultural Foundation, the Scanlon Foundation launched the *Mapping Social Cohesion* research program in 2007. It is a longitudinal study that has tracked the state of social cohesion in Australia.

The foundation also conducts special studies such as; English language competency in Australia; the settlement experience of recent Chinese and Indian migrants to Australia, and a study of international students to Australia. The work of the foundation is widely acclaimed, and it has made an enduring contribution to social cohesion in Australia at a time when many nations have been experiencing racial, ethnic and religious intolerance and conflict. For Bruce, the master's degree in Applied Social Research he had completed in 1997 at Monash University proved to be a great asset in his ongoing work with the foundation.

Max's academic interests and his love of the United States took him back to California in 1999. He, Mel and Kent moved to Palo Alto in the legendary Silicon Valley and he again lectured at Santa Clara University. Their daughters Keli and Julia, who were now both adults, remained in Melbourne but visited regularly.

The move to the United States was also an arrangement struck as part of the deal with Ross Cooper Lund and NFO, the new owners of MarketMind. They were both based on the east coast but were happy to have Max in the USA within striking distance on the west coast. Max revelled in the vibrant experience of living there during the 'dotcom boom' taking place in Silicon Valley. He, Mel and Kent flirted with staying and their applications for green cards were approved giving them the opportunity to reside in the US permanently. But before they collected the green cards, the calamitous September 11th terrorist attacks, commonly referred to as '9/11' took place. They took heed, relented to the urging of their daughters and returned home to live permanently back in Australia.

Offers for Max to become involved with another two Australian universities emerged around this time. He was already connected with Swinburne University of Technology where Professor John Miller, his former dean from Caulfield Institute of Technology, now head of the Swinburne Graduate School of Entrepreneurship, had invited him to the honorary position of adjunct professor. At Santa Clara, he had met Professor Chris Miller, an American national who had been working at Bond University, Australia's first private, not-for-profit university. Based at Robina on the Queensland Gold Coast, Bond was opened in 1989 and is named after Alan Bond, the West Australian rogue entrepreneur who provided the land for the university campus. Chris Miller, who was returning to Bond University from California, offered Max an adjunct professorship in 2001. The work was largely research and could be done from Melbourne, but Max and Mel were interested in the Gold Coast and soon acquired an apartment there. Escaping Melbourne's cold winters had special appeal, especially for Max. He was therefore able to work in close proximity to the Bond campus every winter.

The third appointment was at the University of Wollongong which describes itself as 'a research-intensive university'. Another of Max's former colleagues, Professor John Rossiter invited Max to join a team that in 2006 prepared a government-sponsored public information campaign to combat a potential pandemic of avian influenza, more commonly known as 'bird flu'. The World Health Organisation had recommended that nations prepare for a pandemic by reducing public panic through information and education campaigns. Fortunately, the anticipated pandemic did not hit the nation, so the campaign was never needed. However, the university did retain Max's services as an honorary principal research fellow for several years.

In 2003 and 2004 Max consulted in an honorary capacity assisting the CEO of SCOPE (formerly the Spastic Society of Victoria) to reposition the not-for-profit organisation from exclusively catering to the needs of cerebral palsy sufferers to a necessary broadening of the organisation's service focus.

His greatest commitment, however, was triggered by Max's mother, Myrtle, who in 1999 died a slow and torturous death from a neurodegenerative disease. She had asked for her doctor's assistance to hasten her death but this was not to be as the doctor would have been risking a penalty of up to 14 years in prison. Max was determined to do what he could to change that law. He became an active member of Dying with Dignity Victoria (DWDV) in 2005. DWDV was founded in 1974, formerly the Voluntary Euthanasia Society of Victoria, and is a law reform and education organisation that pursued 'public policies and laws which enhance self-determination and dignity at the end of life.'[11] Max joined the board of the organisation and recruited ex-MarketMind staffer Neil Francis who was elected president of the organisation and head of the World Federation of Right to Die Societies. The advocacy at that time took place amidst a growing dissatisfaction by the community with existing laws, and a forceful commitment to the cause by an increasing number of high-profile people. Max thought the law reform objective would be achieved in two to three years, but it was to be well over a decade before they won the right for Victorians to ask for medical assistance to end their life if they were suffering and terminally ill.

Ironically, in 2010 Max was diagnosed with Parkinson's disease. He says he doesn't advertise this but nor does he hide it. He admits it slowed him down, but he continued to work closely with Neil and high-profile advocates such as Dr Rodney Syme, the former Northern Territory Chief Minister Marshall Perron and media personality Andrew Denton. Persistence began to pay off and they saw the first seeds of their efforts in 2015 with a victory in the Victorian Parliament's upper house. The Legislative Council voted to hold a public inquiry into end of life choices. Max had made his own, powerful submission to the inquiry. The final report was tabled in June 2016 and an intensive emotional battle took place to get the Voluntary Assisted Dying Act 2017 passed by both houses of the Victorian Parliament. Despite fierce opposition, the Bill passed and is now law in Victoria. Max's role was acknowledged by DWDV by the award of the 2018 *Rodney Syme Medal*.

His mission didn't end there though. His efforts continue, now aimed at changing the law in the other state parliaments and nationally, so that all Australians will have the same legal right to ask for the assistance his mother was denied. Will he use the new Victorian law himself when the time comes? 'Maybe' he says. 'Who knows until you reach that point? The important thing is the peace of mind you get knowing it is there if you do need it.'

Since MarketMind was sold much has changed in the world. In market research, the internet has changed data collection and the decline of the landline phone has complicated methods of representative sampling. More than two decades on, there is also much excitement about 'big data' and AI – not just in market research but in data analysis generally. Much IT investment today is going towards managing and maintaining systems that aim to reveal patterns, trends, and associations, especially relating to human behaviour and interactions.

Has the change been for the better? It's arguable that it has not. Bruce has the last word. He has remained actively involved in the research discipline through his work for the Scanlon Foundation and has had an overview of the challenges brought about by the communication and technological revolutions that have characterised the last 20 years. To him, the most obvious things that contribute to the 'not for the better' arguments are:

> Online non-probability panels are now the dominant source of market and social research data. They are popular because they are fast and relatively inexpensive. But they do not provide representative samples of the total population and suffer from self-completion mode effects. The questions and questionnaires typically lack content, context and structure. They produce quick and cheap headline fodder but contribute little

to understanding and accurate representation of what they purport to measure.

Telephone, at one time the dominant mode of data collection, now requires a dual frame sampling solution to address the concurrent rapid decline in fixed land line and rapid growth in mobile telephone only households The absence of a representative population sample frame for mobile phones further exacerbates the difficulty of obtaining reliable survey results. And the problem of increasing non-response rates adds to the methodological challenges confronting front-line researchers today.

What 'big data' can do is increasingly important but at the same time it is hyped and stretched, so much so that it has hijacked the focus. It has overwhelmed the search for meaning in data. Searching for meaning in data requires many things: storage and analysis tools that provide quick and easy access; time to sift through the haystack to find the needle; expertise to know what to look for and recognise it when found; and an audience prepared to pay for and then listen to the end result. MarketMind had this capability. It had developed world best data storage, analysis and access tools, and was on track to transition into AI. It had clients who recognised the value of the product and were prepared to pay for the service. And it had people invested in providing the best information possible. I don't see evidence of this today.

In summary, MarketMind created the means by which market and social intelligence could be rapidly delivered to end-users. It is arguable whether anything better exists today. Sutherland Smith/MarketMind was ahead of its time!

16

THE REFLECTIONS OF OTHERS

The many people who had worked with Bruce and Max and those who were closely associated with Sutherland Smith and MarketMind businesses were asked, for inclusion in this book, to reflect on their experiences from the early 1980s to the late 1990s. Market research, like any professional services business, is totally reliant on the quality of the people it attracts. There is no plant and equipment, no product manufacturing facilities. The people who worked with Max and Bruce were a remarkable group of professionals. Many soared to new heights after the sale of the two businesses and some launched their own, successful firms. Former clients were also asked for their reflections and they readily replied.

The Sutherland and Smith offspring were also asked to share some of their recollections of their fathers' enterprises.

Dianne Gardiner
Coder & Research Executive
1992-1997
Founder, CEO
Latitude Insights
Chief Executive Officer
Bastion Latitude

My most vivid memory of Sutherland Smith relates to a hand-drawn poster Peggy Duell put next to me on the wall of the coding department which read *Monster in Training*. Peggy was by no means a monster, but she certainly knew how to speak her mind and she took me under her wing and decided I needed to find my voice and give a little attitude back. So, I was to become her *Monster in Training*. Today we would never be able to refer to someone in a workplace in this way! And so, with gentle encouragement, Dianne, the quiet mouse in the corner, came out of her shell, found her voice, grew the confidence to speak her mind and eventually became a valued researcher. Who knew that I would eventually become a pretty good 'quallie!' Thanks Peggy for stirring up the monster in me! This is a small but classic example of how Sutherland Smith helped develop team members' potential.

Sutherland Smith was my first 'real' job and it laid the groundwork for what has been a fabulous career in market research and gave me the foundation to one day set up my own MR business. Thanks Bruce and Max for inspiring me from my first day to my last at Sutherland Smith.

Omnia Holland
Director
Sutherland Smith Vic
1988-1996
Founder/Managing Director
OmniCom Research Pty Ltd and Curious Cat Research Group

Sutherland Smith was all about 'how do we do this better?' It was always a collaborative culture. You were given lots of responsibility and I would happily work sixteen-hour days. Bruce and Max were concerned about the hours I put in, but I was always happy to do so.

Jane Rodwell (nee Marks)
Market Research Manager
Gillette Australia

Gillette management decided to create a market research position and wanted me to head it up. We had no one within the organisation in Australia to train me. Our Marketing Director Ian Jackson had a very good working relationship with Max and Bruce and the three arranged for me to work with Sutherland Smith for three months to learn the 'trade'. Gillette owned multiple brands at the time and were conducting a lot of research. I didn't consider that it was an unusual arrangement at the time. In my time at Sutherland Smith, I was considered part of the team and just fitted in. I worked on jobs for some of their major clients and moved around in those three months to be involved in quantitative and qualitative research projects and analysis of results.

I have very good memories of my time there and continued to have a great working relationship with Sutherland Smith for as long as I was in the research position (I was subsequently transferred to Gillette Asia-Pacific). Sutherland Smith felt very inclusive and the staff were collaborative. Bruce and Max were open to new ideas and everyone was encouraged to think creatively. It was clear that they did things properly – there were no shortcuts. They were all about excellence.

Dale Chant
Programmer
MarketMind/NFO Worldwide
1991-2004
Co-founder, Director
Red Centre Software

I recall being ridiculed by the secretaries because I was an MS-DOS neophyte. I didn't know how to change drives from A: to B: – and I was ragged mercilessly by Peggy.

I had the freedom to come and go as I pleased. The art of programming required large slabs of pure thinking and uninterrupted time, better obtained by working at home than at the office. Seventy-hour weeks were the norm.

The typical frustrations of programming (poor briefs leading to useless apps) were never in evidence. We deployed DevOps at its finest. Our users were right there, and if they didn't like something, they could explain why, and we fixed it immediately. Progress was very rapid and tightly focussed.

Max and Bruce played a pastoral role which went well beyond their obligations as employers.

Simon Friend
Business Development Manager
MarketMind
1996-2001

I joined MarketMind having been one of the early users in Kuala Lumpur when I was Managing Director of Frank Small & Associates Sdn Bhd. Max and Bruce asked me to join them as their business development person establishing new licensees and supporting existing users.

I was based at home in rural New Zealand and spent a lot of my time on the road throughout Asia, South America and Europe. One particular year stands out – in 2000 I had 97 international check-ins and 300 hotel nights – thank goodness it was before 9/11!

To me there were two MarketMinds – the Sutherland Smith MarketMind and the NFO MarketMind. The Sutherland Smith MarketMind was our baby – we loved it, nurtured it, developed it and enjoyed it. NFO I believe never really understood (or wanted to understand) the product. They had no idea of markets outside the USA or of different time zones. I would be woken at 3 am in a Hong Kong hotel by some middle-management executive with a question which they could have looked up themselves.

THE REFLECTIONS OF OTHERS

Mark Solonsch
Account Director
Sutherland Smith
1991-1995
Consumer Research Lead, Medibank

There is today a very vibrant alumni of Sutherland Smith. In recent times I have worked, or been in touch, with Liane Ringham, Dianne Gardiner, Monica Greenwood, Stephen Prendergast, Omnia Holland and others.

I have often thought about what makes a professional services organisation – market research or any other – successful. There are two key factors: it must have a combination of technical skills and people skills. Max was technically brilliant, and Bruce had incredibly good people skills.

The quality of tracking research that we did at Sutherland Smith back in the early 1990s is still not matched to this day. As a client I am constantly bemoaning the fact that I can't get the quality of tracking that I'm looking for.

Liane Ringham
Managing Director
Sutherland Smith (NSW)/Sutherland Smith Ringham
1992-1998
Founder & Chief Executive Officer
Inside Story Knowledge Management

When Bruce and Max appointed me to run the Sydney office, they trusted me and never micro-managed me but were there when I needed them. It was a very successful partnership and there was never any disharmony. Since then I've not been able to find a business partnership that has been as effective or as successful.

Lawrence Ang
Senior Consultant and Tracking Manager
Sutherland Smith (NSW)/Sutherland Smith Ringham
1995-1999
Associate Professor, Marketing
Macquarie University

I remember quite vividly when Max gave a seminar at the Australian Graduate School of Management on advertising tracking. I was finishing off my PhD at the time and thought Max's seminar was simply brilliant. That was when I decided to try to go back into the industry. At the end of the seminar, I asked him for a job! He was such a genuine old soul, and still is. He directed me to get in touch with the Sydney office. And as they say, the rest is history.

Working at the Sydney office was such a buzz, especially when Max visited us, or when I visited the Melbourne office. I still remember the countless number of debates we had about what he wrote for *AdNews*, or what measures should come first in a tracking survey, or how MarketMind software could be further refined, or how our database could be milked for more intelligence, and so forth. It was also satisfying when we consistently won our pitches against Millward-Brown, and we had all the blue-chip clients ranging from Qantas, the Australian Tourist Commission, Smith Chips to Fuji-Xerox. What a buzz!

Peggy Duell
Administration Director
Sutherland Smith/MarketMind
1987-2005

I first met Max when he was in the Jolimont Terrace office. At the time I was working with Nationwide Research Services. It was sometime later when I met Bruce. I recall Martin Van Herk lighting his cigars in Max's office and we had to fumigate the building after Martin departed. I was doing interviewing and general administration for Nationwide. All our data entry and coding of our questionnaires was being done in Sydney, and Max decided to have it all done in Melbourne so that we could do the quality control. I learnt to do the coding – my introduction was a pile of questionnaires each with a yellow sticky note attached and four lines written on each that said; 'ad, item, brand, message'. I worked with Sutherland Smith and then MarketMind for nearly twenty years. I was there until we closed MarketMind in Australia. I was the one who was the last out and locked the door behind me.

Romano DelBeato
Researcher
1993-1996
Co-founder DelBeato Young

During a lunch at the Rosstown Hotel I compared moving from Coles Myer to Sutherland Smith somewhat undiplomatically to disembarking from an aircraft carrier onto a small dinghy. Bruce retorted that he hoped they would rate at least as a destroyer. Whatever the craft, I fitted in quickly and developed warm and productive relationships with everyone. The company had an array of skilled and experienced people and offered demonstrably valuable products – quantitative and qualitative. The staff, as well as clients, understood this, and the company culture was characterised by a healthy pride and an underlying confidence. It approached the ideal cultural mix of research-driven aspiration and practical economic efficiency, a balance of two forces which had been very lacking in my previous employments.

Neil Francis
Account Director
MarketMind
1995-2000

What I liked was there was an absence of egoism from the top. What a delightful, professional bunch of people they were! While I was attached to MarketMind and not part of the Sutherland Smith mainstream, there was always a lot of banter in the corridors and the lunchroom.

Stephen Prendergast
Researcher
1987-1992
Founder & Managing Director
Prescience Research

It was when Sutherland Smith was a small business that I gained an appreciation of personal responsibility. You were the one who had to solve the problem – whether it was a computer system malfunction, an interpretation issue, needing to understand something in the market or solving a field problem – you had to deal with it. Often you didn't learn these skills in a big company.

There was also the rigour of cause and effect. If you initiated something you should see an outcome. If you didn't get an outcome perhaps you didn't do it well enough. This came from analysing continuous tracking data. Ad hoc research that existed before continuous tracking tended to not have the tools to analyse cause and effect. Return on investment is all about understanding cause and effect. It was my exposure to continuous tracking that taught me this rigour.

Monica Greenwood
Researcher
1993-1997

When I look back, I remember a great bunch of people who didn't take themselves too seriously and knew how to have fun while being mindful and serious about the work. Everyone worked very hard but knew how to have some fun. I recall having to finish a report before the end of the year. I managed to get it done by five o'clock on Christmas eve and then having to fax it to the client. I suspect it wasn't read until after the Christmas break but at least I met the deadline.

John Wigzell
UK affiliate
1992-1998

I was in Australia on a short secondment to learn as much as I could about the MarketMind product. Bruce and Max were wonderful hosts and took me into their families. I returned for many years to visit them. They introduced me to the ways of the antipodes, explained what it was to be a 'Pommie bastard' and tried to teach me how to sing 'Advance Australia Fair'!

Peter Butler
Marketing Manager
Beecham, Ardmona Fruit Products & Australian Dairy Corporation
1977-1989

I first met Bruce in London when he came to the work in the research department of Masius Wynne Williams Advertising agency, who were our main agency in the UK. I was working for Colgate-Palmolive in the UK as a research executive in the market research department.

My overriding impression of Sutherland Smith was of a consummately professional market research company whose problem-identification and solution processes were second to none. The people were a delight to work with both on a professional and personal level. Though we have gone our separate ways over the years I feel we have always had great respect for each other on both a professional and personal basis.

Ian Jackson
Marketing Director and senior international director, Gillette
1979-2001

Of all the researchers I dealt with over the years – and there were many – Max was by far the most impressive. I first worked with him before he and Bruce got together. He had intellectual horsepower and he always had integrity, independence and clarity of thought. I have great admiration for the work he and Bruce did.

Dr Paul Smith
Son of Bruce & Sue

I did four weeks of work experience with Sutherland Smith in Carnegie – just after the sale. It was a good grounding in building spreadsheets and statistics software, which was enough for me to focus my attention on getting into medicine! I particularly remember one thing dad did which was to go say 'good morning' to everyone. It was a very simple thing to do, which conveyed a very important message – I value your contribution. It's something I try to do in my work (even though some of my employees drive me to the point of insanity).

I remember dad often going to Sydney. But at least I always got a comic book when he returned. I do the same thing for my kids when I go away.

Keli Sutherland
Elder daughter of Max & Mel

I recall when I was about nine, sitting for hours at the kitchen table with mum and dad and drawing graphs with coloured marker pens. They were used for overhead projectors. These days you can create them in about twenty seconds! Because Sutherland Smith worked for Gillette, we were always getting samples; every time there was a new shampoo on the market, we would get to try it.

Dad got into computers very early. He realised the value of computers and, from around 1986, we always had one in our house. Few of my friends had a home computer so they would come around and play games on ours.

On Saturday mornings we would go shopping with dad. Everyone knows that when you shop with dad you buy different things than when you shop with mum – doughnuts and other junk food for example!

Julia Sutherland
Younger daughter

Some of my earliest memories are of the time we lived in Kent, Ohio. These, and our other trips to the United States, are happy memories.

It's only in the past five years that I have developed a greater understanding of what dad and Bruce achieved in business. It's since I've been running my own business that I now have a deepened appreciation of the magnitude of what they achieved.

Dad was always incredibly busy and yet he was there for us. We did some amazing things as a family in the holidays – we went on great trips; we went water-skiing and he took me to see the Harlem Globetrotters several times. As I get older, I become more and more grateful for being part of a happy, fully functioning family unit.

Kent Sutherland
Son of Max & Mel

Dad was often telling us about the psychology of advertisements. He would often tape television programs at night. I would come into the lounge room the next morning to see him fast forwarding through the programs to get to the ads. I would want to watch the show, not the boring ads!

If any of us kids said we liked a particular ad, it was never good enough to say it was funny or entertaining, dad would ask, 'What brand is it for?' I managed to name the right brand no more than 10 per cent of the time.

I recall that dad was always very busy with his work and would spend up to sixteen hours a day, but he always made time to spend with us kids.

Georgia Smith
Daughter of Bruce & Sue

I thoroughly enjoyed access to the stationery store for my artistic endeavours. I have fond memories of endless reels of butcher's paper I turned into various masterpieces.

When I got a bit older (about nine) and fancied myself as a choreographer I utilised the storage space at Carnegie for creating my own ballets.

Dad did a lot of day trips to Sydney. In the 90s there was a lot of overseas travel. Whilst we missed him dreadfully, we always benefited with amazing gifts on his return...or even better, getting to go with him. We spent one summer in the UK – which I think was intended for work – however I have memories of following the Australian cricket team around the country.

Dad worked very hard, would sometimes miss dinners and was always up very early, but it never felt like he was missing from the family.

ACKNOWLEDGEMENTS

We thank many people who have contributed to the creation of this book. The memories of former Sutherland Smith and MarketMind colleagues, clients, relatives and competitors were priceless in helping us reconstruct and recall events and activities over the years. Most have been named and quoted in the manuscript. They are:

Lawrence Ang, Dale Burrows, Peter Butler, Dale Chant, Romano DelBeato, Peggy Duell, Neil Francis, Simon Friend, Dianne Gardiner, Monica Greenwood, Bill Harper, Omnia Holland, Ian Jackson, Shelby McIntyre, Stephen Prendergast, Rod Preston, John Rossiter, Liane Ringham, Kevin Sharp, Mindy Simpson, Elick Teitelbaum, John Wigzell, Patricia Williams, Judy Winikoff and Michael Winikoff (Kingsley's widow and son).

To all the other people who were part of the Sutherland Smith/MarketMind story, we are well aware of the contribution they made, even though they were not interviewed for this book. They know who they are and we thank them too.

Thanks also to the Sutherland and Smith offspring – Keli, Julia and Kent Sutherland and Paul and Georgia Smith.

And finally, a special acknowledgement to Mel Sutherland and Sue Smith.

Both were deeply involved in the businesses and therefore able to fill many significant gaps in the preparation of the manuscript. But perhaps most importantly, they supported their husbands in so many ways, including the nurturing of happy, stable family environments. Given the absence of their husbands for lengthy periods, the heavy home lifting fell to Mel and Sue and the true extent of their achievement is evident in the testimonies of their children.

FURTHER READING

Advertising and the Mind of the Consumer:
What works, what doesn't and why
Max Sutherland
Allen & Unwin: 2008 (third edition)

Some Reflections on the First Fifty Years of Market Research in Australia 1928-1978
W. A. McNair editor (typescript, copy held on ADB file, National Library of Australia)

Principles of Integrated Marketing Communications
Lawrence Ang
Cambridge University Press: 2014

The Complete Guide to Australian Gambling
Mark Solonsch
Wrightbooks: North Brighton:1991

Advertising and Promotion Management
John R. Rossiter and Larry Percy
McGraw-Hill: New York: 1987

ENDNOTES

1. Van Herk was banned from 'managing a corporation' for two and a half years from April 8, 1992. Australian Securities Commission letter.

2. *Harvard Business Review* is published six times a year by a publishing house that is wholly owned by Harvard University. It was first published in 1922 and retains its status as a leader in its field of publishing learned articles on leadership, management and other business issues.

3. The research was commissioned by the author of this book.

4. *Advertising and the Mind of the Consumer:*
   What works, what doesn't and why
   Chapter 10: sub-heading: *Negative roles or characters*

5. While the hotel was not heritage listed, it did have a historical link to Carnegie. When the suburb was first established, it was known as Rosstown after William Ross who constructed a railway line through the area in the 1870s that was never used. Ross' many business failures led to the renaming of the area to Carnegie in 1909.

6. *The Complete Guide to Australian Gambling*: Mark Solonsch: Wrightbooks, 1991

7. Treasurer Paul Keating made his widely quoted – and long-remembered remark – at a press conference on November 29, 1990. It was followed by decades of strong economic growth and prosperity.

8. *New responsibilities in the NFO MarketMind Melbourne office*: A 2000 internal announcement by Richard (Rick) Lund. While the announcement was undated, it referred to Peggy's appointment commencing June 1, 2000.

9. NFO Worldwide Inc: Press release issued November 13, 1998.

10. Wikipedia

11. Dying with Dignity Victoria website: www.dwdv.org.au

www.ingramcontent.com/pod-product-compliance
Lightning Source LLC
Chambersburg PA
CBHW072049290426
44110CB00014B/1615